ARTHUR MILLER

DENNIS WELLAND

OLIVER AND BOYD
EDINBURGH AND LONDON

OLIVER AND BOYD LTD
Tweeddale Court
Edinburgh, 1

39A Welbeck Street
London, W. 1

First published 1961
Reprinted 1964
Reprinted 1966

Printed in Great Britain for Oliver and Boyd Ltd
by Robert MacLehose and Co. Ltd, Glasgow

CONTENTS

ACKNOWLEDGMENTS

Thanks are due to Mr Arthur Miller for permission to reproduce all quotations from his works made in this book.

Acknowledgments are also due to MCA Artists Ltd, and to the following publishers and periodicals for permissions granted in connexion with works by Arthur Miller: *Atlantic Monthly* ("The Family in Modern Drama"); Cresset Press Ltd (*Collected Plays*); Harcourt, Brace and World, Inc., and Victor Gollancz Ltd (*Focus*); *Harper's Magazine* ("Monte Saint Angelo" and "The Shadows of the Gods"); *Holiday* ("A Boy Grew in Brooklyn"); Meridian Books, Inc. ("Please Don't Kill Anything"); *The Nation* ("A Modest Proposal for the Pacification of Public Temper"); Mr E. Seaver and A. A. Wyn, Inc. (*The Man who had all the Luck*); *Tulane Drama Review* ("Symposium on *Death of a Salesman*"); Viking Press Inc. (Adaptation of *An Enemy of the People*, *A View from the Bridge*, 1955, and *The Misfits*).

Acknowledgments are also due to the following publishers for permission to quote from the works indicated: Chatto and Windus, Ltd (Aldous Huxley, *Music at Night*); William Heinemann, Ltd, and Farrar, Straus and Cudahy, Inc. (Mary McCarthy, *Sights and Spectacles*); Simon and Schuster, Inc. (William H. Whyte, *The Organization Man*); Yale University Press (Eugene O'Neill, *Long Day's Journey into Night*, and David Riesman, *The Lonely Crowd*).

The photograph on the front cover is reproduced by permission of The Radio Times Hulton Picture Library.

Finally, I wish to thank my friend and colleague, Mr B. C. Lee, and my wife, both of whom read this work in manuscript and made valuable suggestions for its improvement. In obtaining copies of stories and articles published only in ephemeral magazine form I have been greatly helped by the United States Information Service Library in London, to whose unfailing and practical interest in such projects any student of American literature in this country must be continually indebted.

D.S.R.W.

PREFACE TO THIRD IMPRESSION

Since the first publication of this book two further plays by Arthur Miller have appeared and critical commentary on his work has proliferated. Fully to take account of this would have necessitated a re-writing and expansion of this book too substantial to be practicable, although its basic premises and its evaluation of plays before *After the Fall* are still valid. I have therefore left the Bibliography in the form in which it was first published, but the reader may wish to supplement it by reference to the following, *inter alia*:

After the Fall: first published in *Saturday Evening Post* (1 February 1964) to coincide with first stage production at Lincoln Centre Repertory Theatre, New York; issued in book form by Viking, New York, 1964, and Secker & Warburg, London, 1965.

Incident at Vichy: New York (Viking) 1965; London (Secker & Warburg) 1966.

EISSENSTAT, MARTHA TURNQUIST: "Arthur Miller, A Bibliography" in *Modern Drama* v, May 1962.

HOGAN, ROBERT: *Arthur Miller*, Minneapolis (University of Minnesota Pamphlets, No. 40) 1964; London (Oxford University Press).

HUFTEL, SHEILA: *Arthur Miller: The Burning Glass*, New York (Citadel); London (W. H. Allen) 1965.

LEWIS, ALLAN: *American Plays and Playwrights of the Contemporary Theatre*, New York (Crown) 1965.

D.S.R.W.

August, 1966.

CHAPTER I

THE FACTS

Few dramatists have been more articulate on their own behalf than Arthur Miller: his various prefaces, lectures, articles, and interviews listed in the bibliography at the end of this book already provide a formidable critical commentary on his five major plays and on the theory of literature that underlies them. "Never trust the artist. Trust the tale," warned D. H. Lawrence. "The proper function of a critic is to save the tale from the artist who created it."[1] Arthur Miller is less in need of such salvation than are many of his contemporaries, but an independent commentator may hope to show Miller as not only an important dramatist but also an important *American* dramatist whose work occupies a significant place in a tradition of American literature. Such a viewpoint has been challenged by Miller himself:

> My approach to playwriting and the drama itself is organic; and to make this glaringly evident at once it is necessary to separate drama from what we think of today as literature. A drama ought not to be looked at first and foremost from literary perspectives merely because it uses words, verbal rhythm, and poetic image. These can be its most memorable parts, it is true, but they are not its inevitable accompaniments.[2]

To the extent that this is more than a truism ("Plays should be approached through the theatre, for which they are intended, rather than on the printed page"), this statement is that of a playwright speaking to playwrights. The theory of language which underlies it is the basis of Miller's best work, and its validity is evidenced by the abortive revival, in the English theatre of the nineteen forties, of a verse-drama that was suicidally literary in its aims and methods.

That the dramatist ought not deliberately to aim at writing within a literary tradition does not, however, necessarily isolate him from such a tradition, despite the vigorous counter-assertions of a young American theatre critic, Robert Brustein, explaining "Why American Plays are not Literature":[3]

> The typical American playwright is encouraged to write, not by the pull of literary ideals, but by the stimulus of successful Broadway plays. . . . Making his friends mainly within the theatrical profession, he rarely ventures out of it to have his mind refreshed.

Miller is the only dramatist whom he exempts from this stricture, and even then only partially:

> Since he is an artist with substantial gifts and a real affection for ideas, it seems a waste that some of his own plays should suffer from the very defects he observes in the plays of others; and it is very possible that these defects might have been avoided or overcome if there had been more opportunity for debate, conversation, and intercourse with his equals in the other disciplines.

This seems an unexpected complaint in a society where the creative writer has, in the universities at least, a more established role than in any other country, and where the opportunity for intellectual intercourse provided by the writers' conference, the public lecture platform and the middle-brow magazine (such as that in which Mr Brustein is writing) is more likely to prove a tempting distraction to the writer than to meet a long-felt need. Even if it is true, however, that the dramatist avails himself of these, limited as their value may be, less fully than the novelist and the poet, and even if he is thus isolated from his peers, to phrase the problem in this way is only to associate him more firmly with an American literary tradition of long standing. Ever since Hawthorne prefaced *The Scarlet Letter* with "The Custom House" and Edgar Allen Poe created such nightmares of alienation as "The Fall of the House of Usher," the American writer has tended to see himself isolated in an inimical society with which he is constantly at war. I do not accept this as a fair or complete definition of Arthur Miller's position, but I am prepared to believe that his constant pre-occupation in his plays with people who are, in one way or another, denied a sense of community has its origins in his own experience and his own social attitudes. For Miller, just as much as for Hawthorne or Henry James, "it's a complex fate, being an American"; and, like their novels, all his plays are original and thoughtful enquiries into the nature of that complexity.

Miller was born in New York City on 17 October 1915, and has published an account of his early years under the title "A Boy grew in Brooklyn."[4] This is a delightful exercise in nostalgia, full of racily-told anecdotes, but, as far as Miller himself is concerned, not very informative. We hear more about his grandfather, who is amusingly and affectionately presented as a "character." He "had been a blunt sort of Germanic businessman all his life; had had a factory of importance for many years, [but] with the depression his income was gone." Young Miller consequently rose at 4.30 a.m. to deliver bread for the local bakery before going to school, and school seems to have left on his memory an impression less vivid than the occasion when the bicycle overturned and he got all the loaves back into the wrong bags.

I know that in later years, when I began to publish, my old high-school teachers looked through their records in an attempt to remember me, but not one of them could. I was, in fact, thoroughly invisible during the entire four years, and this is by all odds my most successful accomplishment so far. Because the idea all of us subscribed to, was to get out onto the football field with the least possible scholastic interference, and I can fairly say we were none of us encumbered by anything resembling a thought.

Of Miller's family (other than the grandfather) we learn very little, except that his father, who was still living in 1955, had a lively sense of humour, and, it appears, joked with the neighbourhood children in very much the way that Joe Keller does in *All my Sons*. We can sense, too, something of the atmosphere of the Brooklyn in which Willy Loman brought up his two boys, but the article is in other respects characterised by a reticence that is discernible in most of Miller's published references to himself. In fact his father, Isadore Miller, manufactured ladies' coats and was a successful shop-owner before the slump. The family comprised, in addition to Arthur, an older brother, Kermit, and a sister Joan, six years younger, who subsequently became an actress, taking the surname of Copeland.[5]

Miller graduated from high school in 1932, but was unable to go on to college as "nobody in the house was in possession of the fare." The alternative was obvious, and he accordingly worked for two years in an automobile-parts warehouse at $15 a week in order to pay his way to college. This is exactly what Bert does in *A Memory of two Mondays*, which explains Miller's fondness for that play ("Nothing in this book was written with greater love").[6] Having saved enough for one semester, he entered the University of Michigan, and was only enabled to complete his course with financial aid from the National Youth Administration and with a salary earned as night editor of the *Michigan Daily*. He studied economics and history, and quickly became disillusioned in both—but then he had not chosen Michigan out of academic enthusiasm so much as "because I heard they gave writing prizes there."[7] The honorary degree which the University of Michigan conferred on him on 16 June, 1956, cannot have been an award more welcome to him than the writing prizes he won as an undergraduate. The winning of the first of these (for $250) is best described in his own words:

In my sophomore year I won the Avery Hopwood Award in drama with my first play, which is noteworthy because it was written in four days during Spring vacation. Since I had only seen two plays—and those in my childhood from which I remembered nothing— and had read about three others, I could only decide to end the acts by asking a friend how long an act took. I adopted his estimate and won the award.[8]

Whether this is Miller's modesty or whether there was unusually little competition among budding dramatists at Ann Arbor that year is immaterial: this image of the self-taught dramatist pulling himself up by his own boot-straps inevitably caught the American imagination and is promptly amplified in the same account:

For the past four years [this was written in 1944] he has written radio plays, worked in a box-factory, been shipfitter's helper in the Brooklyn Navy Yard.

Five years later John Chapman introduced Arthur Miller to readers of *The Best Plays of 1948–49* not only as the author of the prize-winning *Death of a Salesman* but as one who

has held such tiring jobs as truck-driver, waiter, crew-man on a tanker, and even now spends a few weeks each year working in a factory so he will remember what it feels like to stand on one's feet in one place eight hours a day.

A legend dies hard: not only does Mr Chapman add, for full measure, that Miller has four acres in Connecticut "where he built his work shack with his own hands," but even in 1960 an English newspaper account of Miller on location with John Huston for a new film emphasises his down-to-earth adaptability. He plays baseball with the camera-men ("looking comparatively professional in a golfing-cap") and wins the admiration of the experts (" 'Mr. Miller knows a lot about horses,' volunteered one of the cowboys").[9]

This image of Miller is not a fictitious one, however, even if its projection is at times a little naïve. Not only do the plays suggest an author with an extensive first-hand acquaintance with a variety of ordinary employments, but they attest to the acquiring of that knowledge the hard way. Miller was growing up during the Depression in America and no other single factor is more important than this in determining his work. "It was a good time to be growing up," he has said, "because nobody else knew anything either," and his other references to his experiences of the period are in that key:

> I happened to have withdrawn my twelve dollars to buy a racing bike a friend of mine was bored with, and the next day the Bank of the United States closed. I rode by and saw the crowds of people standing at the brass gates. Their money was inside! And they couldn't get it. And they would never get it. As for me, I felt I had the thing licked.
>
> But about a week later I went into the house to get a glass of milk and when I came out my bike was gone. Stolen. It must have taught me a lesson. Nobody could escape that disaster.[10]

None the less, it was the Depression that gave him his compassionate understanding of the insecurity of man in modern industrial civilisation, his deep-rooted belief in social responsibility, and the moral earnestness that has occasioned unsympathetic—and often unjust—criticism in the age of the Affluent Society. Before he graduated from college he had collected another Avery Hopwood Award and the Bureau of New Plays prize. In 1944 came a Theatre Guild prize of $1,250, and in 1947, by winning the Drama Critics' Prize for the season's best play of American authorship, *All my Sons* set the pattern that has led to witticisms about Miller as the "most-prized" American dramatist.

But this makes it too simple a success-story, for Miller had already written eight or nine of what he calls "desk-drawer plays" before this, only one of which had been produced in the professional theatre. Significantly, this had been called *The Man who had all the Luck*, and its story, as Miller defines it, is of a young man who

is daily becoming convinced that as his desires are gratified he is causing to accumulate around his own head an invisible but nearly palpable fund, so to speak, of retribution. The law of life, as he observes life around him, is that people are always frustrated in some important regard; and he conceives that he must be too, and the play is built around his conviction of impending disaster. The disaster never comes, even when, in effect, he tries to bring it on in order to survive it and find peace.[11]

This theme (the play itself I shall discuss in the third chapter) is clearly rooted in the nineteen-thirties. It belongs to an age of privation and disquiet, of economic insecurity, when wealth seems the product of luck rather than merit, and when guilt is the response proper to the decent-minded possessor of money. This is not unexpected in a dramatist who, after leaving college, had worked with the Federal Theater Project. Essentially a creation of the Depression, the Project was closed down, because of the improved condition of the national economy, before Miller had a play for it to produce, but he must have been with it long enough to be inspired by its enthusiastic left-wing sympathies that had experimented with such techniques as the "Living Newspaper" and had produced such playwrights as Clifford Odets when the nineteen-thirties were at their depth. Any self-identification Miller may have seen in the play's title must, however, have been shattered when *The Man who had all the Luck* was withdrawn after only four performances on Broadway.

Nor has Miller had all the luck matrimonially either. A marriage in 1940 to Mary Slattery, whom he had met at college, brought a son and daughter, but it ended in divorce in June 1956. Had Miller's second marriage been depicted in one of his plays, it would have been attacked either as too improbable to be convincing or as too contrived and allegorical (and, to be fair to him, it is not the sort of situation he would invent). That an intellectual should marry a glamorous film actress who had just divorced a baseball star is conceivable in the theatre of Tennessee Williams, but such a union might have suggested to him developments more sensational than any that accompanied Miller's marriage to Marilyn Monroe. For the four years of its duration the partnership appeared to achieve a stability that made its break-up even more unexpected than was its beginning.

Miller married Marilyn Monroe on 29 June, 1956, at which time he was very much in the public eye for other reasons. A week earlier he had appeared before a Congressional Investigating Committee in circumstances that deserve to be restated. The trouble had begun in March 1954 when the State Department refused him a passport to attend the opening of *The Crucible* in Brussels, announcing its belief that he was supporting the Communist movement. This Miller denied at once with categoric terseness. The activities of the Congressional Un-American Activities Committee were daily attracting more notoriety to the name of Senator McCarthy, and the liberal press was doing what it could to preserve sanity. Characteristically, Miller published in *The Nation* in July 1954 "A Modest Proposal for Pacification of the Public Temper."[12] This suggested, with intensely-felt irony, that everyone should, on his eighteenth birthday and every two years thereafter, present himself for Patriotic Arrest. While in prison he would be classified either as a Conceptual Traitor (one who had engaged in conversations "not Positively Conducive to the Defence of the Nation against the Enemy" or had "failed to demonstrate a lively, visible, or audible resentment" against such conversations) or as an Action Traitor (one who had attended meetings of groups proscribed by the Attorney General). With Swift-like thoroughness he allowed for a third small class of Unclassified citizens which would be mainly composed of those committed to institutions for the insane or homes for the aged and infirm, members of the F.B.I., those who are not registered borrowers in any public library, veterans of the War Between the States, and *most* children. Still following Swift he blandly anticipated the objections. To say

that this is exactly what the Russians do, is emphatically not true. I insist that no Russian goes to jail excepting under duress, force, and unwillingly; hence, he loses his liberty. But under this Act the American Presents himself to the prison officials . . . without loss of liberty, his most precious possession, because he presents himself with Love in his Heart, with the burning desire to Prove to all his fellow-citizens that he Is an American and is eager to let everybody know every action of his Life and its Patriotic Significance. It may as well be said that if an American boy is good enough to fight he is good enough to go to jail for the peace of mind of his Country.

This was hardly calculated to earn the restoration of his

B

passport, but no further action appears to have been taken
against him at the time.

In 1955 the New York City Youth Board heard rumours
of Miller being a potential candidate for investigation and
consequently delayed ratifying a contract for a film-
script they had commissioned him to write illustrating
the Board's work with street gangs. In December a
decision to ratify the contract was no sooner announced
than it was cancelled, though the Board made clear that
it was not passing judgment on Miller's loyalty or artistic
powers. Then, on 21 June 1956, came the interview with
the investigating committee. This was the *New Republic*'s
editorial comment on it, after castigating the unscrupu-
lous attack made by counsel:

> But Miller wouldn't fight back. He had never been
> under Communist discipline, he said, and he had
> explored—and rejected—the party's professed love for
> creative artists. Also he stayed cool and unemotional.
> We had never seen Miller before. He is impressive.[13]

Miller's statement was accepted by the committee and on
7 July the *New York Times* reported the renewal of his
passport for a six-month period (instead of the usual two
years), but he was not yet out of the wood. Almost a
year later, on 31 May 1957, he was declared guilty of
contempt of Congress for his refusal, at his hearing, to
name others whom he had seen ten years earlier at
Communist-sponsored meetings of writers. Miller's firm
stand on this issue was to be expected of the author of
The Crucible; it was made with a quiet dignity that earned
him respectful applause in *The Commonweal* and elsewhere.[14] No punishment was imposed in respect of the
contempt, and in August 1958 his conviction was unani-
mously reversed by the Appeals Court. A few months
before this reversal he had been elected to the National
Arts and Letters Institute by a courageous decision that
was doubtless intended to recognise not only his literary

merits but also his significance as a liberal in a society
where liberalism was not easy.

Another aspect of his career in 1956 that may have
surprised some of his readers was the announcement that,
four days after the civil ceremony, he and Miss Monroe
were remarried in the Jewish faith. There had been very
little in his writings to suggest that he had been born and
brought up in this faith, although one critic has claimed
to detect a deliberate "de-Semitising" process at work in
the changes in some of his earlier plays.[15] I am inclined to
believe that the lack of emphasis on Jewish elements in
his writing, as well as the use that he makes of them on
two occasions to be discussed later, is a logical aspect of
his liberalism rather than an attempt at concealment.
Miller would be quite likely to feel that a militant
Hebraism would be as illiberal and unproductive an
attitude in some ways as its antithesis, and inimical to
his more usual spirit of tolerance. Matthew Arnold
might have interpreted the didacticism of Miller's
writing as a characteristic of Hebraism, in his terms,
rather than of Hellenism, but when one thinks of present-
day American Jewish writers Miller's is certainly not one
of the names to come first to mind, even though in 1959
he was honoured by the Hebrew University in Jerusalem.

However, this book is concerned with Miller as a writer,
and with his place in American literature. I say literature
(*pace* Mr Brustein) rather than drama for two reasons.
Attempts to identify any meaningful American dramatic
tradition before Eugene O'Neill are chauvinistically
pious and wishful thinking, while the developments in
American drama since O'Neill began writing, exciting as
many of them have been, have hardly coalesced into
anything as homogeneous as a tradition.[16] In any case
Miller's dramatic antecedents are cosmopolitan: he has
more in common with Ibsen, Shaw and Brecht than with
O'Neill, Odets or Thornton Wilder (Miller himself has
said that "the most radical play" he ever saw "was not

Waiting for Lefty but *The Madwoman of Chaillot*," and that
he "had always been attracted and repelled by the bril-
liance of German expressionism after World War I").[17]
Nor has Miller been "encouraged to write . . . by the
stimulus of successful Broadway plays" even to the extent
that Mr Brustein, for all his exceptions, implies. It would
be foolish to minimise the impetus that the success of
Death of a Salesman must have given his writing, but, after
all, that was twelve years ago now, and he has only
published three more plays in that time. Each of them,
however, has differed significantly from its predecessors,
so that one is inclined to think of Miller as the E. M.
Forster of the theatre, writing only when he has something
he wants to say and refusing to cash in on an easy popu-
larity by repeating himself. From what he has said in
print about his own methods of working it is clear that he
does not write quickly nowadays and that he is not easily
satisfied with what he writes. It is not poverty of invention or lack of ideas that inhibits him, but an excess of
self-criticism coupled with a restlessness of intellect.

Moreover, Miller has never thought of himself exclusively as a dramatist, though he obviously finds in the
theatre his greatest challenge and his greatest excitement.
When *The Man who had all the Luck* was printed in 1944
an editorial note introduced him as having

> just returned from a month's trip through eight Army
> camps to gather material for a picture about the Army
> and [he] is now in Hollywood writing the screen
> picture.

This material also formed the basis of a novel, *Situation
Normal* (1944), which is now out of print, and after the
failure of the play on Broadway he published another
novel, *Focus* (1946) currently available in a paperback
reprint. Throughout his career he has published a
number of critical articles in periodicals (as complete a
list as possible appears as an appendix to this book); he

is a short story writer of some distinction, a cinema-script writer, and his most recent appearance is as a contributing editor of a twice-yearly literary magazine, *The Noble Savage*. The *New Republic* journalist, writing of him as he appeared before the Congressional committee, defined him as "the passionately self-exploring, artist-genius type." It is a crude description, but not inaccurate.

REFERENCES

1. *Studies in Classic American Literature*, 1922; Repr. in *The Shock of Recognition*, ed. E. Wilson, 1943.
2. *C.P.*, pp. 3–4.
3. *Harper's Magazine*, Oct. 1959, pp. 167–72.
4. In *Holiday* magazine, Mar. 1955, beginning at p. 54.
5. *New York Times*, 1 Jun. 1957, p. 8.
6. *C.P.*, p. 49.
7. Biographical details in this chapter are collated from such sources as the introductory notes to the publication of his plays in volumes like the annual Burns Mantle *Best Plays of 19—*; or the notes on contributors in periodicals in which he has published prose.
8. *Cross-section*, 1944, ed. E. Seaver, p. 556.
9. *The Guardian*, 3 Nov. 1960, p. 8.
10. "The Shadows of the Gods," in *Harper's Magazine*, Aug. 1958, p. 36. The cycle anecdote is also told in the article quoted above, n. 4.
11. *C.P.*, pp. 14–15.
12. *The Nation*, 3 Jul. 1954, pp. 5–8.
13. *The New Republic*, 2 Jul. 1956, p. 2.
14. *The Commonweal*, 14 Jun. 1957, pp. 268–9. See also Mary McCarthy, "Naming Names: The Arthur Miller Case," in *Encounter*, VIII (May 1957), pp. 23–5.
15. Henry Popkin: "Arthur Miller: The Strange Encounter," in *The Sewanee Review*, LXVIII (1960), p. 37. Popkin also mentions an earlier article in *Commentary* on Jewish elements in *Death of a Salesman*.
16. The best account of these developments accessible in this country is Joseph Wood Krutch, *American Drama since 1918*, rev. edn., London 1957.
17. *C.P.*, pp. 37, 39.

CHAPTER II

THE FICTION

With all the acumen of hindsight it is not difficult to see in *Focus* an adumbration of many of Miller's later themes and the beginnings of his flair for dialogue, but any reviewer of the time who failed to forecast from this the emergence of a major dramatist cannot be blamed. *Focus* is a competently constructed novel which handles a simple and uncomplicated plot with directness and a compelling clarity. In some respects, however, its straightforward-ness is a handicap to it as a novel, for it fails to suggest an actual world with the density and the complexity that we expect of the novel. Its New York setting is only lightly sketched in; there is little or no description beyond the simplest, and that is atmospheric rather than visual:

> At that hour a man can pitch a tent in the Wall Street neighbourhood and sleep soundly, hardly hearing a single footfall or automobile on the streets. The buildings were locked up tight, like tall vaults. The stores were dark. As far as the eye could see the city was dead, and the green smell of the sea hovered along the sidewalks.[1]

The most sustained piece of description has overtones of Steinbeck and Dos Passos; it attempts, by a laconic collocation of disparate instances, to communicate the impression of a drought. Commentary is reduced to a minimum and restricted to the non-emotive statement of a generalised truth:

> For nearly forty days the city had had no rain. It is an insidious pacifier, rain; the people stay at home and

the pages of the precinct blotters do not turn so often. But when the sky stays as blue as it did this summer, day after sweltering day, and the humid air chokes a man out of his sleep, it is the streets and stoops of the city that become populated and the authority of the family disintegrates for a time. . . . In Brooklyn there was an exceptionally heavy invasion of stinging flies and it was difficult to buy screens because of the war. Two enormous amusement parks burned down and several piers caught fire. People were afraid to go to the amusement parks after this and afraid to go to Coney Island, but they had to go, and they went, and they were always worried. Even the subways started acting peculiarly. In one week alone three trains were discovered speeding along on absolutely the wrong tracks. For nearly forty days the city had had no rain.[2]

The "poker-faced epic" quality that this prose attempts with its simple sentences and its resonant flatness of tone counteracting its Olympian viewpoint is as Steinbeckian as is the device of repeating the key opening sentence at the end or the hinted anthropomorphic concept of the subway. The absence of the feeling for the natural world and for the animal symbolism that mark *The Grapes of Wrath* is not due solely to its urban setting. The significance of events for Miller, much more than for Steinbeck, is the directness of their impact on human beings, and his interest in men does not so readily aggrandise itself into a preoccupation with Man. The single, sudden step from the drought to the disintegration of the authority of the family is an easy and a natural one for Miller to take, but it is taken, in this context at least, with fewer political overtones than in Steinbeck's novel which takes not just a larger version of the same step but fundamentally a less human one. Steinbeck's characters, for all their idiosyncrasies and individuality, are constantly mythologised into Mankind. Miller's, in this novel and even in

Death of a Salesman, are first and foremost ordinary people. His is the dramatist's interest and *Focus* is a dramatist's novel, relying less on narrative and description than on characterisation, dialogue and a succession of situations rising in a crescendo to a climax.

It is the story of a New York office worker whose Jewish appearance makes him the victim of an anti-Semitism with which he has some sympathy, and its concern is with the process by which he brings into focus his own views and his own insights. This is neatly symbolised by his reluctance to acquire the new spectacles that his failing eyesight demands; when he is forced into buying them it is the spectacles that accentuate his Jewish appearance and precipitate his victimisation by a world that he can at least see more clearly. Focusing implies a narrowing of the vision, however, a concentration on a more limited area, and although this justifies the pattern of the novel—the tension increasing as the vision narrows—it does lead to some distortion of perspective. The concentration on Lawrence Newman is a dramatic technique of considerable power but he is not fully enough visualized in his domestic setting, and his mother, with whom he has lived as a bachelor for over forty years, remains a figure more nebulous and ineffectual than is adequately explained by her condition of semi-paralysis. The refusal to explore her reaction to the wife whom he so unexpectedly brings home is a significant narrative evasion, for it leaves out of account entirely a pressure on Newman that needs to be emphasised, not ignored. The theme of this novel, as much as of his plays, is the one that Miller defines in the question: "How may a man make of the outside world a home?"[3] and for Newman this is a problem connected with his family life more integrally than Miller allows in the novel. Up to this point in the story he has tried to do it by self-deception and wish-fulfilment dreams. Like Sinclair Lewis's Babbitt, Newman has dreams of an ideal woman, but where Babbitt's fairy girl is a romantic hankering after youth by a married man with a family, Newman's more earthy woman ("She was large, almost fat . . . her thighs and her hollows nearly touching his hand")[4] is plainly the creation of frustrated sexual desire far more serious in its implications. Similarly, where Babbitt's automobile is a prestige symbol and a means of transport, Newman's attitude to his car, which the war has forced him to lay up, is more complex:

> Without admitting it, however, he enjoyed the car much more now when it was on blocks, for it is well known that rust is a terrible menace to an unused machine.[5]

The weekend care and maintenance that he lavishes on it (generally doing "each Sunday what the manufacturer had advised doing twice a year") is undertaken in a spirit different from the family pride which the Loman boys bring to the polishing of Willy's Chevrolet. It anticipates much more Faulkner's description of the American who

> really loves nothing but his automobile . . . having nowhere to go in it himself and even if he did he would not go where scratch or blemish might deface it, spending all Sunday morning washing and polishing and waxing it because in doing that he is caressing the body of the woman who has long since now denied him her bed.[6]

Whether or not Faulkner is right in elevating the automobile into "our national sex symbol," there is a definite, if not fully worked out, suggestion behind this passage in *Focus* that it is a sex symbol for Newman who for the rest of the week finds it "a terrorizing experience to sit in full view of the stenographers."[7]

Nothing in the novel is more successfully or more movingly depicted than Newman's essential littleness, meekness and hesitancy. His anxiety to please his employers, his fear of dismissal, and his constant worrying, all foreshadow similar anxieties in Willy Loman, whose interview with his employer is scarcely more painfully conveyed than is the corresponding scene in the novel. But Willy's brash salesmanship makes his liaison with the woman in Boston convincing in a way that Newman's marriage is not. Gertrude's quasi-Jewish appearance does not motivate this in an entirely satisfactory way, even when it is allied to her resemblance to his dream-woman, and the situation is not improved by playing down the impact on the domestic life of mother and son that her arrival might be expected to have.

This may not be a failure of the imagination but a limitation deliberately imposed upon it. The impulsiveness and irrationality of some of Newman's self-destructive actions link him more closely with the irrationality of the world in which he lives, an irrationality which the novel seeks to establish as a destructive principle in a civilisation which, brought into focus, is seen as a barely-refined savagery. The authority of the family, the microcosm of civilisation, is so insecure that its disintegration can be threatened by a change in the weather or by a chance impulse. To make the central figure of a novel about anti-Semitism a Gentile who is mistaken for a Jew is an attempt to keep the theme itself in focus, to reveal anti-Semitism for what it is instead of generating a factitious indignation on behalf of a persecuted Jew to whose suffering a more emotional, even sentimentalised, response could be very easily stimulated. It is a more remarkable achievement when we remember Miller's own origins. Newman is the little man at the mercy of forces whose nature he only dimly recognises and to which he only gradually and with difficulty develops a hostility. His own prejudices, his inertia, his vacillation, and his meekness, all restrict very successfully the appeal that Newman makes to the reader's sympathy, so that his victimisation is seen as partly self-induced, and anti-Semitism is seen as growing less from the exercise of positive evil than from the failure of positive good. The novel opens with Newman in his room at night watching a woman being beaten up and excusing his non-intervention with a succession of glib reasons; only in the final paragraph of the novel, when he voluntarily identifies himself with the Jews, does Newman behave in any way like a hero. Miller's success in this novel is achieved through a technique of Brechtian "estrangement"[8] whereby the reader is denied the consolation of emotional identification with a character the better to understand a situation as a whole: the emotion is reserved for the issue, not squandered on fictitious characters. Newman's story is firmly subordinated to these considerations and his character is developed only in relation to them, but this gives Miller excellent opportunities of devising situations that he was to re-work later in the theatre. The family resemblance between Newman and Willy Loman has been touched on already; the latent irrational prejudices that flare out, in conjunction with an almost cynical opportunism, as a twentieth-century New York pogrom, are recognisably akin to those that provoke the Salem witch-hunting of *The Crucible*. As in *A View from the Bridge* (the title of which carries implications similar to those of *Focus*) the twin themes of responsible integrity and betrayal for motives only dimly understood are balanced against each other, and Newman, like Eddie Carbone, "allowed himself to be wholly known." The essential difference, of course, is that Newman has tried "to settle for half" and abandoned the attempt in the absence of an Alfieri to demonstrate its desirability. There is something "perversely pure" about his final alignment of himself with Finkelstein and the Jewish cause, but Miller does not recognise the perversity here as clearly or as maturely as in the later work. The end of the novel suggests that he sees it as a code by which Newman can live, or at least as a code less unequivocally destructive than Eddie's.

To turn directly from *Focus* to "The Misfits," a short story that Miller published in 1957, is to become aware of the framework, not only chronological but thematic, into which his major dramas fit. At first this cowboy story, with its clipped, Hemingway idiom and its preoccupation with physical action, seems an unlikely development for Miller, even a retrogression. In the Introduction to the *Collected Plays*, he had spoken of the artist's interest in "process," but there it had seemed to mean some more psychological process such as that by which Lawrence Newman comes to accept responsibility for anti-Semitism or Joe Keller is brought to pass judgment on himself; it had not seemed to anticipate this detailed concern with the physical process by which three mechanised cowboys, equipped with a plane, a truck, and ropes anchored to heavy tyres, round up wild mustangs.

> Gay whirled his loop over his head and the truck came up alongside the stallion whose lungs were screaming with exhaustion and Gay flung the noose. It fell on the stallion's head and, with a whipping of the lead, Gay made it slip down over his neck. The horse swerved away to the right and stretched the rope until the tire was pulled off the truck bed and dragged along the hard clay. The three men watched from the slowing truck as the stallion, with startled eyes, pulled the giant tire for a few yards, then reared up with his forelegs in the air and came down facing the tire and trying to back away from it. Then he stood there, heaving, his hind legs dancing in an arc from right to left and back again as he shook his head in the remorseless noose.[9]

Miller's grasp of the techniques involved here is achieved by imaginative sympathy rather than by zealous journalistic research, and never suggests something "got up" for the occasion in the way that, for example, some of Kipling's stories in *The Day's Work* do.

The graphic vividness of this writing, heightened only occasionally by an image ("Quickly the sky flared with true dawn like damp paper catching fire, and the shroud of darkness slipped off the little plane"), emphasises the resemblance between this story and the many others that have made the hunting story almost a *genre* of American fiction. The paradigm, of course, is *Moby Dick*; the most complex modern equivalent is Faulkner's *The Bear*, and the most popular exponent of the form, from *In our Time* to *The Old Man and the Sea*, is Hemingway. Generally these are stories of initiation, and the hunt becomes a reversion to the primitive, a ritual by which man is brought into conflict with elemental forces of nature and from which he emerges purified and strengthened to renew his battle with the civilised life from which the hunt has provided a temporary and welcome withdrawal. In *The Old Man and the Sea*, the hunt, which for the reader becomes an analogue of life,[10] is for the old man life itself, the means and the end of existence, but for the boy, who apprehends it imaginatively, it is a vicarious initiation. In *The Bear*, the terrain over which the hunt takes place and the racial intermixture of Ike McCaslin's mentors constitute an inescapable reminder of the problems of ownership, responsibility, and inheritance, into which he is being initiated, the hunt thus symbolising the fulfilment of the inalienable past.[11] All these stories illustrate the truth of W. H. Auden's comment that, for Americans:

Nature is the dragon, against which St. George proves his manhood. The trouble about that, of course, is that if you succeed in conquering the dragon, there is nothing you can do with the dragon except enslave it, so that there is always the danger with a wild and difficult climate of alternating, if you like, between respecting it as an enemy and exploiting it as a slave.[12]

A rejection of exploitation is one of the reasons for Ike McCaslin's ultimate renunciation of his inheritance in *The Bear*, but that renunciation is, for many readers, inadequately distinguished from evasion and denial of responsibility. Miller's story seems to spring from a recognition similar to Auden's, but to his characters the McCaslin renunciation is not a possible solution.

Exploitation is the keynote of their activities; they even remind themselves to water the mustangs immediately before sale so as to increase their weight—an important consideration because the horses are to be sold for canning as pet-foods. To the realisation of this their conversation constantly and uneasily returns: they console themselves with the reflexions that "Somebody's goin' to take them if we don't," and "They ain't doin' nothin' up there but eatin' out good cattle range. The cow outfits shoot them down if they see them," but their uneasiness remains:

> Gay said "I'd a soon sell them for riding horses, but they ain't big enough. And the freight's more than they're worth. You saw them—they ain't nothin' but skinny horses."

This economic argument is the conclusive one: roping these mustangs is the last job available to them, and "if it ain't this, it's wages." Variants on the phrase "It's better than wages" run chorically through the story, but it acquires an apologetic, embarrassedly shame-faced tone with every repetition. What sounds at the beginning like an assertion of sturdy independence has become by the end an indictment of the times and of the speakers. These are the misfits, but they are not being sentimentalised as the outdoor men who are to be admired for their inability to fit into an urban commercial society. They are just as much misfits on the plateau among the mountains, and the final irony of the story lies in their kinship with the horses they hunt; of the stallion Gay says

"He ain't nothin' but a misfit. . . . You couldn't run cattle with him; he's too small to breed and too old to cut. . . . They're just old misfit horses, that's all."

The sterility of their existence is further pointed by their references to Roslyn, the woman in the town with whom Gay, forty-six and separated from his wife, cohabits. Herself a misfit ("She would go back east one day, maybe this year, maybe next"), she exists in the story only in Gay's thoughts and as a challenge to his sense of security: he expects her to "razz them about all the work they had done for a few dollars" and to be sorry if she knows they have brought in a colt for slaughter. Above all, he is constantly suspicious of her relationship with his young colleague Perce, whom he suspects of being her lover. But Perce is even less secure in his attitude to life than Gay. He is twenty-two and a less confident rope-thrower than Gay, whom he obviously respects ("Hell, Gay, you are the most misfitted man I ever saw and you done all right"): but in one respect he is of greater interest, for we have met him before.

Perce is living the part of Biff Loman's life that is briefly mentioned in *Death of a Salesman*:

> . . . it always turns out the same. . . . It's why I came home now, I guess, because I realized it. This farm I work on, it's spring there now, see? And they've got about fifteen new colts. . . . And whenever spring comes to where I am, I suddenly get the feeling, my God, I'm not gettin' anywhere! What the hell am I doing, playing around with horses, twenty-eight dollars a week![13]

Perce has perhaps achieved more independence than Biff, but at the end of the story, in the truck on the way back to town,

> Perce spoke, sitting up in his seat. "I want to phone my mother. Damn, I haven't called her all year." He

sounded angry. He stared out the window at the mountains. He had the memory of how the colt looked and
he felt an almost violent wish for it to be gone when
they returned.

The hunt has not been an initiation for Perce; it has
served merely to confirm his sense of misfittedness,
whereas initiation implies the discovery of a role to fit
into. The sudden half-guilty recollection of family ties
is the impulse that has always sent Biff Loman home to
New York but for Perce it prompts only the immediate
exclamation: " 'You know something, Gay? I'm never
goin' to amount to a damn thing.' Then, suddenly he
laughed." Perce can laugh where Biff cannot, because
Perce has not tried to settle for half, and because Perce
has found companionship with another misfit. (Gay calls
it "a bravery between them.")

This story shows a considerable technical advance on
his earlier fiction, and as he has spent three years turning
it into a film-script for John Huston he obviously attaches
some importance to it. He has now republished the original story together with an interesting version of the
film-script in novel form.[14] The original has been altered,
not merely to provide a role for Marilyn Monroe as
Roslyn, but to leave Perce once more as lost as Biff
Loman at the end, while Gay and Roslyn head for home
together. It also keys in some elements from another short
story, "Please don't kill Anything",[15] which is themati-
cally linked with "The Misfits" by its concern with man's
predatory raids on the animal kingdom. This time it is a
fishing story which, in one sense, begins where *The Old
Man and the Sea* finished. Fishermen are winching their
nets in to the beach—there is again the well-described
process, and again it is a process brought up-to-date by
mechanisation—where the landing of the catch is watched
by a man and a girl. Like the woman-tourist at the end of
Hemingway's story, the girl has no understanding of the

fisherman's life and the caught fish are to her only an appeal to sentiment, not a symbol of man's prowess. Distressed by the exploitation which leaves the unwanted coarse fish dying on the sand, she makes her companion throw them back into the sea, which he does to his own embarrassment and the amusement of the fishermen. He tries to leave two of the sea robin,

> feeling, somehow, that if he let those two die on the beach she might come to terms with this kind of waste. For he had had to open the window at home, once, to let out a moth which ordinarily he would have swatted, and while part of his heart worshipped her fierce tenderness toward all that lived, another part knew that she must come to understand that she did not die with the moths and the spiders and the fledgling birds, and now, with these fish.

The girl, however, is adamant, and he throws these two back in a scene of quiet comedy unlike anything else in Miller, for each time he throws one in a stray retriever on the beach fetches it out:

> "Well?" he said to her, "there you are. There's a whole conspiracy against these two fish. This guy was trained to help man; man has to eat and something's got to die, Puss. . . ."
>   As he spoke a silvery minnow slid out of the mouth of the sea robin at his feet. "Look at that now!" he yelled. "See? What about *that* little fish?"
>   "Yes!" she said, like an admission.
>   "You see? The victims make other victims."
>   "Well, hurry, throw him back anyway."

The homily is lost on her, but she saves the fish by distracting the dog's attention, and the two go off, hand in hand, the man happy at having gratified her whim, the girl laughing, "with the woman part of her that knew of

c

absurdities," at the prospect of the rescued fish living to see their children grown up.

What may sound in summary like a piece of flabbily humanitarian sentimentality is in fact something quite different. The slightness of the anecdote is given depth by the combination of the girl's innocence, wonder, and capricious femininity with this element of "quiet comedy." Miller's sense of humour, not often prominent in his work, is here used with a humanity and a sense of proportion that are relatively new. For one thing, it is directed at the moralising didacticism of the man with which the earlier Miller would have more readily identified himself. Here it is not so much rejected as put in its place by the woman's irrational common-sense.

The tenderness for animals that both Roslyn and Puss exhibit is a belief in life that was foreshadowed in one way at the end of *The Crucible*:

Life, woman, life is God's most precious gift; no principle, however glorious, may justify the taking of it.[16]

In its context this speech is not wholly validated, for the tragic irony of that play lies in the irreconcilability of life and principle in that particular situation. The change that appears to have occurred in Miller's work is the recognition that not all situations are equally tragic. Of the film of "The Misfits" John Huston remarked "It deals with people who will sell their work but not their lives"; probably no better definition could be so succinctly given of Miller's work as a whole. His central theme has always been integrity—the integrity of the individual towards himself and towards his fellows—but the cost of that integrity for most of his characters has been life itself. In "The Misfits" there is a difference: Miller himself has said of the film:

There is a change. For a long time now I've wanted to make something of existence. It's tragic—after all,

we all die here—but there's something in between.
Gay and Roslyn will die, but they can face it with
dignity. They can do right, and not be like the jerks. It
may not sound much but it's taken a lot to get me to
that point.

The moralistic overtones of this may recall Faulkner's
Nobel Prize acceptance speech, but its slangy casualness
of expression covers a truth important to the understanding of Miller's work. What it has taken to get him to that
point is, as he says, more than it sounds, but it can be very
clearly traced through his plays.

REFERENCES

1. *F.*, p. 66.
2. *F.*, p. 147.
3. "The Family in Modern Drama," in *Atlantic*, Apr. 1956, p. 36.
4. *F.*, p. 23.
5. *F.*, p. 9.
6. *Intruder in the Dust*, New York 1948, pp. 238–9.
7. *F.*, p. 18.
8. Cp. R. Gray, *Brecht*, Edinburgh and New York 1961, p. 60.
9. In *Esquire*, Oct. 1957, pp. 158–66.
10. Cp. S. F. Sanderson, *Hemingway*, Edinburgh and New York 1961, pp. 113 ff.
11. Cp. M. Millgate, *Faulkner*, Edinburgh and New York 1961, pp. 73–4.
12. "Huck and Oliver," in *The Listener*, L (1 Oct. 1953), p. 540.
13. *C.P.*, pp. 138–9.
14. *The Misfits*, New York 1961. The film was the subject of a full-page feature in *The Guardian*, 3 Nov. 1960, p. 8, and references to the film in this chapter are from this source.
15. In *The Noble Savage*, No. 1, 1960, pp. 126–31.
16. *C.P.*, p. 320.

CHAPTER III

BEGINNINGS IN REALISM

That Miller should not reprint *The Man who had all the Luck* in the *Collected Plays* is hardly surprising, for it is obviously a tiro's play, but it is still an interesting, if unsatisfactory, piece. Its hero, David Frieber, is an orphan in a small mid-Western country town who has been set up modestly in business as a garage mechanic by the generosity of friends. A sudden cold snap enables him to sell all the anti-freeze alcohol he has been talked into buying; the obstacle to his marriage with the girl of his choice is removed for him by the death of her curmudgeonly father in an automobile accident; and the eccentric owner of an expensive car which other garages have failed to repair challenges him to attempt it. With the aid of an itinerant German mechanic who drops in to announce that he is setting up in business in the town, the repair is effected. David is given further financial backing, his business prospers, he buys out the German, takes him into his employment, and launches out into other, and equally successful, enterprises. Convinced, from what he sees happening to his friends, that his luck cannot last, he persuades himself first that he will have no children and then that his child will be stillborn, but the boy is in fact "as healthy as a calf." Meanwhile, to satisfy himself that skill matters more than luck, he has mortgaged everything to start a mink farm. Adverse weather conditions and a delivery of diseased fish threaten the success of the minks' whelping on which everything is staked, but disaster might have been averted were it not that his wife, sensing his superstition, forces him to let them die in order to cure himself:

It's not that they must die. It's that you've got to kill them. . . . I want you to know once and for all that it was you who did it. . . .[1]

A dramatisation of luck is likely to strain coincidence to breaking-point, and by the end of the opening scene, when Hester's father has been killed pushing the car he is too mean-minded to allow David to overhaul—and killed by the very vehicle on the repair of which David's lucky career is to be based—the long arm is being stretched to proportions too simian for many readers. But those who are prepared to accept this amount of luck may well be deterred by the monkey-tricks of the next scene where the arm is extended further to pull more chestnuts out. The orphan David has been given until the following morning to repair the Marmon: he is little of a mechanic and in any case the theme requires him to succeed by luck, not by ability. Along comes Gustav Eberson, who not only diagnoses the fault as soon as the engine is started, but completes the job while David sleeps. We may accept the nocturnal ministrations of fairy-folk in a tale by Grimm, but it is another thing to believe that a newly-arrived garage-proprietor would choose the middle of the night for his first call on a rival and would then be so accommodating as to save the situation for him. This first act is the least happy of the three, for it is also cluttered with a superfluity of minor characters who seem to have moved in from Winesburg, Ohio, and lost something in the process. The crippled store-keeper Shory and David's fuddled aunt serve no real dramatic purpose. The Marmon-owner need not make an appearance at all, and it is prodigal as well as unnecessary to bring Hester's father on the stage for two minutes in order to run him over in the wings as soon as he leaves. It is theatrical tact that is lacking here, and self-confidence. What Miller wants to do is to create the sense of a community, a real town, and he does not believe he can do

it except by crowding the stage with people in a spirit of
mistaken naturalism. There is no real reason why the
opening scene should be a store, but the stage-directions
are meticulous in their cataloguing of the hardware on
display and of the furnishings. In the second scene the
Marmon is actually on stage, its engine is started and the
repairs are begun in full view of the audience, and all in a
seriousness unexcused even by the sense of fun and novelty
that brought Jack Tanner's car on to the stage in *Man
and Superman*. Miller's beginnings are essentially in a
naturalism which only emphasises the improbabilities of
plot and character in this play, and I stress its weaker
elements only to gauge his progress since then.

Despite the fairy-tale element, this play is far more of a
hangover from the nineteen-thirties than either *All my
Sons* or *Death of a Salesman* which have been less justly
attacked on that score. For example, Willy Loman's
manual skill is exercised in the do-it-yourself, odd-jobs-
around-the-house relaxation that has become increasingly
a feature of modern suburban life, but the climactic
speech of this earlier play (already quoted) continues
with Hester telling her husband:

> Whatever it is that hangs over your head, take it in
> your hands and kill it now! Whatever it is, you're
> better, you're greater. . . . Davey, you're a good man,
> good with your hands; you've always been a good man!

The *mystique* attached to "good with your hands" here is
developed by David's survey of his possessions, a few
minutes later, and his explanation of the meaning his
mink have for him:

> Half the quarry's mine; could I build a quarry or half
> of it? The shop is mine with all the tractors there;
> could I build a tractor in a thousand years! I stood
> in the world with money in my hands and everything
> was "mine"! It was not *mine*, nothing is mine but what

I'm good enough to make. Money is a bitch, Hester, it's a whore bitch that'll bear for any man and what it bears can never really be yours. Only these animals are mine. In the whole world they're the only things that would have died if I weren't there to make them live!

If this goes back to Thoreau in its desire for elemental creativity, it does so via the emotionalised agrarianism of Steinbeck's fiction and the nineteen-thirties' veneration for the worker as maker. It is distinguished from Jeffersonian idealism by its shrill anti-monetary bias and its sentimentalisation of man's connexion with animals, both of which recall *The Grapes of Wrath*. There is a similarly Steinbeckian note in the emotionalised stage-directions of this play as, for example, in the scene under discussion:

He turns slowly away toward the open door as though feeling the dying of his mink. She steps away from him as though from a child first learning to stand.

Well-meant indignation and intensity of moral earnestness motivate it, even in its minor aspects. Thus, Shory, the store-keeper, is a war-veteran who has lost his legs and who has been soured both by his disablement and by the irony that it was sustained, not on the battlefield, but after the Armistice when a boiler exploded in a Paris brothel; he has no real relevance to the story and seems to belong with *A Farewell to Arms* rather than to the nineteen-forties. His reiterated opinion that "A man is a jelly-fish washed up on the beach" exists only to be repudiated by the play's moral; it is never adequately explored or developed.

Miller remarks that "far from being a waste and failure this play was a preparation, and possibly a necessary one, for those that followed." This he connects, somewhat cryptically, with his sudden recognition that "two of the characters . . . were logically brothers and had the same father"; and when the play was staged on Broadway David's surname was changed to Beeves.[2] One critic sees this as part of a "de-Semitising" process which he detects in this play and its two successors;[3] be that as it may, it makes our hero part of a family pattern that the reader will quickly recognise. A sub-plot in the play concerns Patterson Beeves, whose life and energy have been devoted to the dream of turning his son Amos into a champion baseball player. David generously arranges for a talent scout to watch Amos in action, and one of the most moving scenes in the play is when the scout turns him down. To Patterson's uncomprehending explanation of the intensive winter indoor training he has devised for the boy, he replies: "Yeah, that's just where you made your mistake, Mr. Beeves"; and when Patterson tells him Amos "doesn't know how to do anything else," his reply is the same: "I guess that was another mistake." By making David Amos's brother, Miller gives Patterson two sons, one of whom he destroys through a misplaced and excessive desire for his success, while the other survives the parental devotion, though he is not unscathed by it. It is the story of the Keller family in *All my Sons* and of the Loman family in *Death of a Salesman*. The parallel to the latter is accentuated by the use of the folklore dream of success through prowess on the games-field, and by the identical terms of abuse ("fake" and "liar") that both Amos and Biff apply to their fathers, although Willy's betrayal of Biff is far more complex and more far-reaching morally than Patterson's of Amos. This is a play about luck; Amos was unlucky in the unfortunate error of judgment his father made in the training, and the parental inculcation of wrong aspirations is not so severely in question.

Ideally, David's brother-relationship to Amos needs fuller exploration than it seems to have got, but Miller apparently perceived its full implications only slowly, and

in the three plays in which he develops the roles of the
two sons his attitude to and interest in each of them
changes remarkably. Of the "destroyed" sons, Amos is
passive, dumb and dramatically uninteresting. Larry
Keller is dead before the play opens, but his recognition
of his father's guilt, conveyed in his letter to his fiancée,
is more articulate and more morally perceptive than
Amos's. Biff is the most "aware" of the three, the most
fully portrayed, and the one whose betrayal disturbs us
most. To the other brother Miller's attitude changes more
sharply. David is the play's central figure and the man
who had all the luck. Chris Keller is prompted by a
stronger moral indignation and is faced with bigger
problems: he has learnt in the War that he can fail, but
he has also learnt to live with that knowledge and to
build on it. He still has a lot of the luck, and he retains
something of David's superstitious guilt, though in his
case its motivation is made more acceptable by his description to his fiancée, Ann, of the death of his company of
soldiers.[4] This idealistic social conscience does not escape
criticism: combined with the luck Chris has, it makes him
the object of an envy and a resentment more true-to-life
than the benevolence David's luck inspired in his friends.
Ann's brother embodies it particularly, but a neighbour
has already put it more caustically ("I resent living next
door to the Holy Family"),[5] and even Ann warns Chris
of his tendency to idealise his friends. In the earlier play
David's effect on people is described by his benefactor
J. B. Feller:

Everytime I set eyes on him something happens to me.
I suddenly feel that everything is possible again.[6]

In *All my Sons* this effect becomes more ambivalent:

SUE, *with growing feeling*: Chris makes people want to be
    better than it's possible to be. He does that to people.
ANN: Is that bad?

SUE: My husband has a family, dear. Everytime he
has a session with Chris he feels as though he's
compromising by not giving up everything for research. As though Chris or anybody else isn't compromising. It happens with Jim every couple of
years. He meets a man and makes a statue out of
him.[7]

J. B. Feller and Jim Bayliss not only stand in the same
relationship to the younger heroes of the two plays, but
they both stand for the same values of good-neighbourli-
ness. The difference between them is not merely that an
external critic of Jim is provided for us in Sue: in *All my
Sons* the claims of family responsibility have become a
much more complex problem, and idealism is judged not
per se but in terms of the conflicts it provokes.

Larry and Chris Keller are much more akin to each
other than are the pairs of brothers in either of the other
two plays, and this is not so much because Larry, whom
we never see, cannot be developed as a character, as
because Chris is the most attractive, the most decent, of
the three versions of that character. Davey is wooden by
comparison, less human and less likable, but, like Davey,
Chris learns a responsible independence, and after his
confession of guilt (quoted above) it is again the woman
who tells him, almost in the words Hester had used:

Because you mustn't feel that way any more. Because
you have a right to whatever you have. Everything,
Chris, understand that? To me, too. . . . And the
money, there's nothing wrong in your money.

In saying that, Ann knows something of his father's guilt
but is realistic enough to recognise that Chris bears no
part of it. The change that the Chris-character under-
goes, however, before his next incarnation is striking.
"Happy" Loman has lost all the conscientious scruples
of David and Chris to become as demoralised as his

brother but in a more cynical way. Happy accepts his father's standards without fighting them, and has the adaptability necessary to make them work for himself. He no longer needs any of the luck: he is the smooth operator who gets what he wants by having the personality to take it. It emerges in his conversation with Biff:

> That girl Charlotte I was with tonight is engaged to be married in five weeks. . . . The guy's in line for the vice-presidency of the store. I don't know what gets into me, maybe I just have an overdeveloped sense of competition or something, but I went and ruined her, and furthermore I can't get rid of her. And he's the third executive I've done that to. Isn't that a crummy characteristic? And to top it all, I go to their weddings![8]

David's luck and self-help have degenerated into helping yourself. Gus Eberson says of David:

> Mr. Frieber is not comfortable unless everybody he knows is as happy as himself. He suffers sometimes from an over-developed sense of responsibility.[9]

The change, in what is basically the same character, from "an over-developed sense of responsibility" to "an over-developed sense of competition or something" is a convenient index to a social change to which Miller is peculiarly sensitive. In David Riesman's terminology it is a shift from inner-direction to other-direction and, as such, is indicative of the patterns of social conformity that Riesman and his collaborators were charting sociologically at about the time that Miller was writing *Death of a Salesman*, although their findings were not published until a year later under a title that Miller might have devised: *The Lonely Crowd*. The change also reflects Miller's maturing disillusion in this David/Chris/Happy character, but, even more, it indicates his growing awareness of the importance of the father-character.

All my Sons is linked to *The Man who had all the Luck* in

more ways than this. Both originated in real-life anecdotes Miller had heard,[10] both have a Mid-Western
setting and atmosphere. The fussily realistic detail of the
set is repeated, but this time it is concentrated into one
location throughout, and an element of symbolism is
introduced by the tree. Similarly the cast-list, though
only smaller than its predecessor by one, is confined to
characters who (with the possible exception of the little
boy Bert) are dramatically relevant, and they are more
skilfully utilised. The advance on *The Man who had all the
Luck* is evident both in theme and technique. The story
is clearly a more important one—an aircraft-engine-
manufacturer with no conscience who supplies faulty
cylinder-heads in wartime is likely to command more
attention and to raise wider issues than a mink-farming
mechanic with a conscience at once too sensitive and too
narrow. Nevertheless, it is primarily at the domestic level
that the problem is explored; the real value of the war
framework lies in its topicality, in the audience-indigna-
tion that is universally generated against Joe Keller, and
in the social tensions and guilt that is set up in his sons.
But there is never any question of these emotions prompt-
ing Chris to any form of political action or public protest
—a point too obvious to need making, except that references to the play too often suggest that it is politically-
directed. What concerns Miller here, as in most of his
plays, is the impinging of the public issue on the private
conscience and the domestic circle of the family. His
achievement here, to put it at its lowest, lies in the verisi-
militude with which he creates not only a convincing,
homely family, but also the sense of the flow of com-
munal life in a suburban neighbourhood. There is a
suggestion of social density communicated here more
skilfully and less obtrusively than in the earlier play: the
Kellers are part of a town in a way that the Friebers
never were. Indeed, a possible weakness of the play is
that the atmosphere of American neighbourliness is

allowed to become too predominant, so that we are not
kept sufficiently aware of the latent hostility to Joe that is
mentioned from time to time.

Joe himself is perhaps too pleasant for the part he has
to play. His betrayal of his partner seems out of key with
his simple geniality and warmth of nature. As with most
of Miller's characters, there is no vice in him, only littleness and his own form of myopia. This is one reason why
I emphasise the myopic Lawrence Newman as the sym-
bolic origin of Miller's dramas. Like Newman, Keller
has difficulty in focusing and is genuinely unable to
visualise the public consequences of what was for him a
private act. To have stopped production when the flaw
was discovered would have endangered the future of the
business that meant security for his family: it was as
simple as that. Keller is no villainous capitalist egged on
by competitive mania in a cut-throat world of business,
nor is he the cynical profiteer deliberately reducing the
margin of safety in order to increase the margin of profit.
Other dramatists would have seen him in this light and
written the play that way. Miller sees him as the simple
man who has got on by energy and will-power but who
is hardly clever enough to know how he has done it. To
this extent he is another David Frieber, a man who has
had all the luck, and there is more than a grain of truth
in his wife's comment, "We're dumb, Chris. Dad and I
are stupid people. We don't know anything. You've got
to protect us."[11] In the play, he is the ordinary man,
surprised that "every week a new book comes out,"
occasionally uncertain of his pronunciation, aggressively
proud of his night-school education, yet moved to em-
barrassed facetiousness by his son's knowledge of French,
and perplexed by a world where "you stand on the street
today and spit, you're gonna hit a college man."[12] Yet
even these traits are only sporadically evident: it is the
man's *bonhomie*, sense of fun, and good nature that pre-
dominate. If we come to accept the idea of this man

deliberately allowing his partner to take the blame for shipping the faulty engines and thinking to patch up his conscience as easily as the flaws were patched up to delay detection—and we do accept it in the theatre—it is primarily because of the dramatic effectiveness with which the climax and *dénouement* are brought about. Only later do we realise that it is in character, that it is the reverse of the coin of which the obverse has seemed so attractive, and that the coin is of smaller denomination than we thought, but none the less still a recognisable part of the currency.

The improvement in dramatic effectiveness may be immediately illustrated from the act-endings. In *The Man who had all the Luck* the direction "Slow Curtain" repeated at the end of most of its five scenes recalls too readily the student-dramatist who had had to ask a friend how long an act ought to be. There is not the climactic use of the curtain that is achieved naturally in *All my Sons* even in the first, relatively slow-moving act. The second act is brought to an explosive but perfectly-timed conclusion, and the superbly-developed tension of the play's ending is blurred only by the bringing of Chris back on to the stage for his mother's final and uncharacteristically wise comment. The impulse to prolong the action of *Death of a Salesman* beyond the death of its protagonist is more defensible than this, if only because the central issue of *All my Sons* is simpler and the suicide of Joe Keller dramatically more self-justifying, for the events leading up to it have been presented with a direct-ness and an increasing tempo that make any alternative impossible. By contrast to Miller's skilful observance of the old unities here, the episodic structure of *The Man who had all the Luck*, with its dramatic confusions, loss of pace, and irrelevancies of character and action, seems almost amateurish. The objection is sometimes made that *All my Sons* is so well-constructed as to be unconvincing, and the delayed revelation of Ann's third-act production of the letter from Larry is instanced as meretricious playmanship. On the other hand, her reluctance to produce it earlier is credibly enough explained by her,[13] and it would not be easy to devise a more economic—or a more telling—method of bringing home the two things essential to the action at that point: the demolition of the mother's dream that her son is still alive and the demonstration to Joe, in terms that he cannot escape, of the consequences of his own conduct. Whether Ann, with that knowledge, would have been quite so sympathetic to Joe earlier in the play is another question, but one that Joe's irresistible geniality and Ann's nostalgia for the past go part of the way to answering, especially as she has earlier accepted the court's verdict that the blame was her own father's rather than Joe's.

The confident certainty of dramatic movement here seems deliberately and successfully counterpoised against the loss of certainty that is the play's main theme. The keynote of the play is its questioning. Dialogue in the theatre is regularly carried on in terms of questions and answers, but in *All my Sons* the questions are in effect dialogue-stoppers. The dramatic power resides in the sort of questions asked and in the inability of the characters to answer them. Particularly prominent in the last act and in the exchanges between Joe and his son, this is observable throughout, and it is responsible for the powerful climax to the second act in Chris's agonised reiteration of such questions as "Where do you live, where have you come from? . . . What must I do, Jesus God, what must I do?" Nothing brings out Joe Keller's bewildered isolation better than this exchange with his wife:

KELLER: Maybe I ought to talk to Ann?
MOTHER: Don't ask me, Joe.
KELLER [*almost an outburst*]: Then who do I ask? But I don' think she'll do anything about it.
MOTHER: You're asking me again.

KELLER: I'm askin' you. What am I, a stranger? I
thought I had a family here. What happened to my
family?
MOTHER: You've got a family. I'm simply telling you
that I have no strength to think any more. . . .

KELLER: Then what do I do? Tell me, talk to me, what
do I do?[14]

A few minutes later, among questions to his son, he inter-
jects the same plea: "Talk to me." This is the bewilderment of a naturally garrulous man who has suddenly
realised the impossibility of communication on the matters
of deepest consequence, and it is a dilemma which the
often-criticised banality of Miller's dramatic idiom is
particularly well suited to suggest. Against these baffled
questions and the clichés of his quotidian conversation
Joe's final statement of the play stands out with an integrity and a force far in excess of its verbal content. His
decision is made and his questions answered by the letter
of his dead son:

MOTHER: You're so foolish. Larry was your son too,
wasn't he? You know he'd never tell you to do this.
KELLER [*looking at letter in his hand*]: Then what is this
if it isn't telling me? Sure, he was my son. But I
think to him they were all my sons. And I guess they
were, I guess they were.[15]

That is almost the only statement in this play of questioning that should be taken at its face value, and its quiet
dignity makes Chris's summing-up ("there's a universe
of people outside and you're responsible to it") superfluous and gratuitously didactic. The other and more
sensational statements must be seen in their immediate
context. "This is the land of the great big dogs, you
don't love a man here, you eat him! That's the principle"[16]
—it is not Miller who says this, but Chris, and Chris the
baffled idealist *in extremis*. Its hysterical note distinguishes

it from the more responsible tone of genuine recognition in Joe's speech, and the play is a social drama, not as an attack on the capitalist business ethic, but as a study of the bewildered common man groping in a world where moral values have become a shifting quicksand, where you ask for guidance from others no surer than yourself, and where the simplest lesson—moral responsibility to others—is the hardest to learn.

It has become a commonplace of criticism to link this play with Ibsen and to see it as another version of, for example, *Pillars of Society*. The comparison is as valid as it is obvious, and Miller's own comments on his attitude to Ibsen[17] do not need elaboration. It may be more interesting, perhaps, to approach the question from another angle and, ignoring chronology for the moment, to turn to Miller's adaptation of *An Enemy of the People*, which was staged in 1950-1. He explains that he undertook this:

> Working from a pidgin-English word-for-word rendering of the Norwegian . . . because I had a private wish to demonstrate that Ibsen is really pertinent today, that he is not "old-fashioned," and, implicitly, that those who condemn him are themselves misleading our theater and our playwrights into a blind alley of senseless sensibility, triviality, and the inevitable waste of our dramatic talents.[18]

As is to be expected, Miller makes three sorts of change: changes in language, in structure, and in ideas. The first is, on the whole, the most obvious and the least important from our present point of view. Not only purists will have their doubts about "Well, what do you say to a little hypodermic for these fence-sitting deadheads?"[19] as an alternative to the more usual versions (*e.g.*, "Don't you think it is high time we stirred a little life into all this slackness and vacillation and cowardice?")[20] But this is an extreme instance, and more usually Miller's dialogue

is racy and modern without being as aggressively collo-
quial as this.

He turns it into a three-act play with two scenes in each
of the first two acts (corresponding to Ibsen's first four
acts) and one in the last (Ibsen's fifth), but for the
reader's convenience I have adhered, in my references,
to Ibsen's division into acts. More important structural
changes are mainly in the nature of abridgments of some
passages of dialogue: Miller complains of

> Ibsen's insistence that his meaning be driven home—
> and from the front door right through to the back, lest
> the audience fail to understand him.[21]

Thus the interviews between Hovstad and Stockmann in
Act II, and between Hovstad, Aslaksen, and Billing in
Act III, are shortened, the pace of Act V is accelerated,
and Act IV (the public meeting) is modified in several
respects. The scene opens differently and less use is
generally made of the crowd, Peter Stockmann wrecks
his brother's presentation of his case expertly and econo-
mically without the help of Hovstad and Billing that
Ibsen gives him, and Stockmann's belief in the evolution
of a natural aristocracy of leaders disappears entirely.

Miller's preface attributes this last omission to his
desire to avoid fascist or *Herrenvolk* implications in the
play that he feels Ibsen did not intend. This is being a
little over-cautious, and it helps to support one adverse
criticism of the adaptation as

> a peversion of the original in that it transformed the
> hero into a conventional modern liberal and thus
> rested the case for him rather upon the supposed
> correctness of his ideas than upon the abstract right of
> dissent even if it be a dissent from what passes among
> the intellectuals for right thinking.[22]

For a writer with Miller's liberal outlook this is perhaps
inevitable, and some of the other instances where he

departs from his original have a similar effect. Thus Billing's statement in Act I, "A community is like a ship; everyone ought to be prepared to take the helm," is "democratised" by Miller into "every man should do something to help navigate the ship"; Stockmann's hope is that the wealth from the springs will help his compatriots to become "more like Men, more like A People"; and the scene in Act III, where Stockmann in boisterous high spirits assumes the Mayor's hat and stick and is then obliged to surrender them, is in Miller's version embellished with the following didactic pomposity:

> I just wanted you to realize, Peter [*he takes off the hat and looks at it*] that anyone may wear this hat in a democracy, and that a free citizen is not afraid to touch it. [*He hands him the hat.*] And as for the baton of command, Your Honor, it can pass from hand to hand. [*He hands the cane to Peter Stockmann.*] So don't gloat yet. The people haven't spoken.[23]

If the collocation of these quotations out of their contexts suggests a campaign-address, other speeches in the play remind us that at the back of such sentiments there lies a long tradition of American literary, as well as party-political, thought. When Stockmann's sons return from school at the end of the second scene, Miller makes them tell their father they have learnt at school what an insect is. He replies:

> You know what I'm going to do, boys? From now on I'm going to teach you what a man is.[24]

The theme of his lessons, presumably, will be Emersonian: "Whoso would be a man must be a non-conformist"; and by implication at least "the abstract right of dissent" is supported, as it is again later when Stockmann insists on the need for the pioneer: "Before many can know something, *one* must know it."[25] Similarly one of Miller's additions to Ibsen is also Emersonian in sentiment if not entirely in expression:

> Oh God, on the wreckage of all the civilizations in the world there ought to be a big sign: "They Didn't Dare!"[26]

The case for conformity is put by the Mayor in conventional terms which anticipate *The Crucible*:

> You have an ingrained tendency to go your own way, Thomas, and that simply can't go on in a well-organized society. The individual really must subordinate himself to the over-all, or [*groping for words, he points to himself*] to the authorities who are in charge of the general welfare.[27]

He can explain Thomas's nonconformity only in terms of vindictiveness and hatred of authority, adding a cliché that acquires on his lips an irony which one hopes Miller intends: "This is the mad dream of a man who is trying to blow up our way of life."[28]

But, as in Ibsen, the last word is with Thomas Stockmann, and this receives a characteristic twist: what had earlier been rendered in some such form as "The strongest man in the world is he who stands most alone" now appeared in this version (or inversion):

> But remember now, everybody. You are fighting for the truth, and that's why you're alone. And that makes you strong. We're the strongest people in the world ... and the strong must learn to be lonely.[29]

It is not only the possibly fortuitous overtones of counsel to the United States on the implications of international leadership that makes this so characteristically American, but the whole romanticisation of the loneliness of the high-principled individual. Not long after Miller had written this, Thornton Wilder published an article entitled "The American Loneliness."[30] Wilder was writing on Thoreau, whom he sees as representative of the American because he is "disconnected from place, distrustful of authority, thrown back upon himself":

> And all his triumphs came from his embattled individualism, from pushing it to the limits that border on absurdity, and from facing—"face to face"—the loneliness consequent upon it. He came back with the answer that life, thought, culture, religion, government—everything—arises from subjectivity, from inwardness. Our sole self is the first and last judge of values, including the values of communal life.

So far it might be Miller's Stockmann of whom he is speaking, and Miller's sense of the topicality of Ibsen's play might be paralleled by Wilder's comment:

> Our interest in Thoreau is precisely that we see one of ourselves fighting, struggling and finally fainting in this inescapable American situation.

In the stage direction for Stockmann's last speech ("with a trembling mixture of trepidation and courageous insistence"), and in the speech itself, there is more than a hint of a sentimentalisation of loneliness closer to Wilder than to Ibsen. At the same time there is a more resilient toughness about Miller's 'thirties-born attitude to this "inescapable American situation," and he would not agree with Wilder that "the evil of community is that it renders us stupid—and cowardly" without recognising that community has counterbalancing advantages. If Joe Keller, for example, is "stupid and cowardly," it is not exclusively or even primarily the fault of society, and his loneliness is that of the weak would-be conformist, not of the iconoclastic pioneer. Neighbourliness is a cardinal virtue in *All my Sons*, and even in *An Enemy of the People* Miller's belief in the value of community comes through almost unexpectedly in Stockmann himself. In Ibsen's Act II the doctor had expressed his satisfaction at being able to do good in his own home town. Miller changes this to:

> You can't imagine the feeling, Catherine, to know that your own town feels like a brother to you. I have never felt so at home in this town since I was a boy.[31]

By this emphasis on "at-homeness" he brings the situation more closely into line with twentieth-century American values. Similarly, at the end of Act I, Stockmann's satisfaction at having done something for the community is transposed into a satisfaction at having "earned the respect of one's neighbours." This brings it uncomfortably close to Willy Loman's desire to be liked, and even to be well liked. The "other-directed" nature of this can also be paralleled in Stockmann's praise of the moderate Aslaksen as "a very sincere man." Riesman's observations are as follows:

> The other-directed man, somewhat sentimental about people, is likely to be quite cynical about legal and political institutions, just as he is about the great game of politics itself. Coupled with this outlook, his concern for sincerity in his political personalities becomes a vice. . . . It is obviously most difficult to judge sincerity. While the audience which uses the term sincerity thinks that it is escaping, in its tolerant mood, from the difficulty of judging skills, it is actually moving into a domain of considerably greater complexity. Just because such a premium is put on sincerity, a premium is put on faking it.
>   Plainly, it is the other-directed person's psychological need, not his political one, that dictates his emphasis on warmth and sincerity.[32]

I think that Miller had seen the truth and the implications of this more clearly and more critically in Willy Loman, who is his own creation, than in his Americani-

sation of Stockmann two years later. Even the loneliness
of the strong, to which Stockmann pays a tribute as near
to eloquence as he ever comes, is not really the strength
of a Thoreau, but the strength of a group, consisting of
the family as nucleus, augmented by the dozen street-
urchins whom Stockmann is going to educate. Miller's
Stockmann is thus making a far greater concession than
his original to what, in *The Organization Man*, William
H. Whyte calls the modern ideals of "belongingness" and
"togetherness." Similarly Stockmann's greater insistence
here that the urchins must be "good and ignorant, absolutely uncivilized" seems to owe less to Ibsen's social
realism than (unconsciously) to Frederick Jackson Tur-
ner's hypotheses about the reversion to the primitive
that he believes took place at the American frontier and
the subsequent climb back up the scale of civilisation.

Miller's debt to Ibsen, then, is not closely ideological,
but what he learns from him dramatically may be seen
from this adaptation even more clearly than from his
comments in the introduction to the *Collected Plays*. His
streamlining of the play, so as to eliminate some of the
ponderousness he complains of in Ibsen, has been
already illustrated, but one minor improvement is made
in the last scene by dovetailing Peter's exit with Kiil's
entrance. In the original they were separated by three
speeches, but their coinciding ironically appears to substantiate Peter's allegation of complicity between Stockmann and Kiil, and Peter's contemptuous snort as he
leaves gives dramatic point to this. Miller also makes
another, and less expected, change by increasing the
element of humour. This is sometimes done by additions
to the dialogue, such as Stockmann's warning to his
brother in the last scene against sitting too close to the
already-broken windows: "Not there. A piece of the solid
majority is liable to open your skull." It is also effected by
making the Mayor a little more comic in his pompous
conservatism, but without playing down his more sinister

characteristics. Rather more use is made of the drunken man at the meeting, and Billing's pseudo-liberalism in Act II also comes in for ridicule by being Americanised:

> Doctor Stockmann, I feel as though I were standing in some historic painting. Goddammit, this is a historic day! Someday this scene'll be in a museum, entitled "The Day the Truth Was Born."[33]

The main change, however, is in the role of Morten Kiil. A new opening to the play has Kiil finishing dinner at the Stockmanns' with Billing. He leaves as the Mayor arrives, but not before he has helped himself, unobserved, to apples and tobacco, and then, with polite shows of refusal, allowed his daughter to give him some more. His miserliness is throughout a source of comedy, and so is his inability to understand Stockmann's explanation of the nature of bacteria (this whole exchange is developed more amusingly and more fully than in Ibsen). Miller does not bring Kiil in to the public-meeting scene at all, which seems in character, and, without minimising his unscrupulousness in the last act, allows him to make his final exit on Aslaksen's arrival with the wry comment: "Too many intellectuals here: I'd better go."

The humour that Miller injects, not unsuccessfully, into Ibsen's play has not been much in evidence in his own, and he is hardly likely to make a great comic dramatist. Such comic touches as there are in this play seem intended, like those in the other plays discussed in this chapter, simply to contribute to the realism of the whole. Although he jokes that Ibsen's plays "have always been set forth with yards of fringe on every tablecloth and drapery," his own version of *An Enemy of the People* only cuts a few inches off that fringe, and his own plays before *Death of a Salesman* belong, broadly speaking, in the same familiarly realistic convention. The sort of notices that *All my Sons* received were favourable in their tributes to his talent and theatrical craftsmanship, but, understandably, not out of the ordinary. Robert Garland in *Journal-American* is representative:

> It says something of moment about something of moment, it says it with controlled emotion and impressive skill. Frequently it is indignant, but always about the real and righteous things.

That a sympathetic reviewer might have made exactly the same comments on an early Ibsen play is not an adverse reflexion on Miller, for there is a perennial value in plays that have something to say and say it with ability; that the play should have been "the play of the year" in 1949 suggests that the native American theatre and its critics were somewhat more conventionally-minded than the post-war European theatre. *All my Sons* is the least original, the least exploratory in theatrical technique, of all Miller's major plays; but, although it is interesting as a preparation for the later plays, it has enough vitality and importance to hold the stage on its own merits. I have seen its essential qualities brought out remarkably by an arena-type production, with the minimum of properties, in a very small hall. The directness of the intimacy of this certainly overcame any suggestion of the stiffness that the play is sometimes accused of, and brought out eloquently the human relationships on which the play is, like all of Miller's, so firmly based. Shorn of its naturalistic setting, it gains rather than loses.

The problem with which Miller has always had to contend is how to keep in dramatic balance his natural ability to create human and sympathetic characters and his tendency to didactic moralisation of his scenes and themes. In the three plays that I have discussed in this chapter the didactic element is not tightly enough reined. The remaining plays all show more enterprise and originality in their experimentation with new means of achieving this balance, while at the same time they progressively widen the scope of his subjects. It is on them that his present reputation rests.

REFERENCES

1. *Cross-section* 1944, p. 550.
2. *C.P.*, pp. 14, 15. (As the Broadway version has never been published, I have not been able to verify whether the text was modified, and have had to assume that, but for the change of name, it remained as already printed.)
3. See above, p. 13, n. 15.
4. *C.P.*, p. 85.
5. *C.P.*, p. 94.
6. *Cross-section* 1944, p. 490.
7. *C.P.*, p. 93.
8. *C.P.*, p. 141.
9. *Cross-section 1944*, p. 518.
10. *C.P.*, pp. 14, 17.
11. *C.P.*, p. 90.
12. *C.P.*, p. 96.
13. *C.P.*, p. 122.
14. *C.P.*, p. 119.
15. *C.P.*, p. 126.
16. *C.P.*, p. 124.
17. *C.P.*, pp. 19–22.
18. *E.P.*, pp. 11, 8.
19. *E.P.*, p. 49.
20. For comparative purposes the translation cited is that of R. Farquharson Sharp in the Everyman Library (London 1911).
21. *E.P.*, p. 12.
22. Joseph Wood Krutch, *American Drama since 1918*, rev. edn., New York 1957, p. 325.
23. *E.P.*, p. 79.
24. *E.P.*, p. 61.
25. *E.P.*, p. 95.
26. *E.P.*, p. 103.
27. *E.P.*, pp. 26–7.
28. *E.P.*, p. 74.
29. *E.P.*, pp. 124–5.
30. In *The Atlantic Monthly*, August 1952, pp. 65–9.
31. *E.P.*, p. 50.
32. *The Lonely Crowd*, Anchor Abridged Edition, New York (Doubleday), pp. 227–8.
33. *E.P.*, p. 190.

CHAPTER IV

DEATH OF A SALESMAN

Discussion of *Death of a Salesman* has always been be-devilled by the question: is it a tragedy? The success of its New York presentation—its 742 performances put it among the fifty longest recorded Broadway runs, and it took both the Drama Critics' and the Pulitzer prizes—did not prevent, indeed perhaps invited, hostility. Eric Bentley, abroad when it opened in February 1949, attacked it on his return and hit hard at everything from the lighting to the language, directing his onslaught particularly at what he saw as the play's conflicting aims:

> The "tragedy" destroys the social drama; the social drama keeps the "tragedy" from having a genuinely tragic stature. By this last remark I mean that the theme of this social drama, as of most others, is *the little man as victim*. The theme arouses pity but no terror. Man is here too little and too passive to play the tragic hero.
>
> More important even than this, the tragedy and the social drama actually conflict. The tragic catharsis reconciles us to, or persuades us to disregard, pre-cisely those material conditions which the social drama calls our attention to. . . . Or is Mr. Miller a "tragic" artist who without knowing it has been confused by Marxism?[1]

Exactly the reverse hypothesis was advanced by Eleanor Clark in *Partisan Review*;[2] she saw Miller as a Marxist who had been confused by tragedy:

It is, of course, the capitalist system that has done
Willy in; the scene in which he is brutally fired after
some forty years with the firm comes straight from the
party-line literature of the 'thirties, and the idea
emerges lucidly enough through all the confused
motivations of the play that it is our particular form
of money economy that has bred the absurdly false
ideals of both father and sons. It emerges, however,
like a succession of shots from a duck-blind. Immediately after every crack the playwright withdraws
behind an air of pseudo-universality, and hurries to
present some cruelty or misfortune due either to
Willy's own weakness, as when he refuses his friend's
offer of a job after he has been fired, or gratuitously
from some other source, as in the quite unbelievable
scene of the two sons walking out on their father in the
restaurant.

The whole play, for Miss Clark, is characterised by

an intellectual muddle and a lack of candor that
regardless of Mr. Miller's conscious intent are the main
earmark of contemporary fellow-traveling. What used
to be a roar has become a whine.

At about the time of the play's opening, Miller himself, interviewed by the New York Times, stressed the
tragic intention:

The tragic feeling is evoked in us when we are in the
presence of a character who is ready to lay down his
life, if need be, to secure one thing—his sense of
personal dignity.[3]

Important as this idea is in Miller's later plays, it was
confusing when associated with Death of a Salesman, for
critics were quick to point out what the play itself
demonstrated—that Willy Loman's sense of personal
dignity was too precariously based to give him heroic
stature. Since then it has become tediously conventional

for the writers of books surveying modern drama to praise the play's social realism but hurriedly to add that, of course, it falls short of tragedy and is therefore disqualified as a "great play." (This complaint is usually associated with strictures on its unpoetic use of language.)

What is irritating about such criticism is its assured conviction that the mixture of social drama and tragedy is unintentional, and its implication that, if Miller had only been clear-minded enough to concentrate on one or the other, a better play would have resulted. Better or not, it would have been a totally different play, and for once the audiences who took the play that was offered to them seem wiser than *genre*-minded critics who wanted something else. Eric Bentley is perfectly right to see it as a play about "the little man as victim," but less right when he seems to prefer the little man to be a victim of only one thing, and to assume that a "social drama" must be a socialist drama. The Marxist plays of Clifford Odets in the nineteen-thirties had rarely communicated a sense of the complex density of the society they criticised, and merely to show the little man as the victim of capitalist big business would, in 1949, have been "picayune," to use one of Miller's own words: Elmer Rice had done that well enough in *The Adding Machine* twenty-six years earlier.

The evidence for a Marxist interpretation of *Death of a Salesman* is, in any case, not very impressive. The scene in which Willy, seeking a change of job, is unceremoniously dismissed can hardly have been intended as the indictment of capitalism that Miss Clark thinks it. Theatrically it is a moving, even painful, scene, but it engenders a mixture of pity and exasperation rather than the indignation that we would expect of "party-line literature." Willy's behaviour is not calculated to enhance his or our sense of his personal dignity: even as we pity him for his despairing reduction of the wage he will settle for, we are exasperated by his inability to see that he is throwing away any chance he may have by his obtuse mishandling of Howard. The central irony of this scene resides in the discrepancy between Howard and our preconceived idea of the capitalist tycoon. This is no ruthless executive callously firing the trusted employee from calculated mercenary motives: it is the "nice guy" forced into a situation that he doesn't know how to handle "nicely" and consequently only making the ugliness of it worse. It is one little man being fired by another little man, Willy being fired by a younger Willy. Howard's callousness is occasioned less by his business acumen than by his absorption in his personal life. The tape-recorder serves two purposes in the scene: when Willy stumbles against it and sets it accidentally into motion it precipitates an hysterical breakdown that symbolises the central theme of the play in Willy's horror at his inability to switch it off—to switch off the recorded past. Whether the past is that of his own sons recorded on his memory and conscience, or that of Howard's son recorded on a mechanical instrument, it is the past, more than capitalism, of which Willy is always the victim. The machine also provides a means of dramatising Howard's ingenuous pride in his children. They are far more real to him than is the memory of his father to which Willy constantly appeals, and his pride in their prowess and their affection for him obliterates any understanding of Willy's plight, exactly as Willy's pride in his sons has blinded him to any recognition of the worth of Bernard. This point is emphasised by Howard's automatic question, "Why don't your sons give you a hand?" and by the immediate introduction of the Ben-*motif* as a further reproach to Willy's vacillatory sentimentality. Moreover, this memory-sequence dissolves into the actuality of Charley's office, where a successful Bernard on his way to professional and social triumphs in Washington unintentionally prompts Willy into another orgy of envious recrimination at everybody except himself.

The irony set in motion in Howard's office culminates in Charley's, for it is Charley, not Howard, who is the nearest thing to the big business-man in this play, and yet Charley is the only person who offers Willy any positive help. The money he advances him and the employment he offers have no strings attached: Willy's acceptance of the one and rejection of the other is the outcome of a very curious sense of personal dignity, but there is no mistaking the truth of his exit line:

> WILLY [*on the verge of tears*]: Charley, you're the only friend I got. Isn't that a remarkable thing?[4]

It is remarkable to Willy not only because he has never had any time for Charley, but because Charley is the exact antithesis of himself. To describe Charley as the Horatio to Willy's Hamlet (as one critic at least has done) is to put it too romantically, but the antithesis is clearly and succinctly drawn by Willy's exchange with Charley over Bernard's success:

> WILLY: And you never told him what to do, did you? You never took any interest in him.
> CHARLEY: My salvation is that I never took any interest in anything. There's some money—fifty dollars. I got an accountant inside.[5]

Charley the successful business-man is the only person who understands Willy the failed salesman, but he understands him in a wholly unsentimental way quite different from the "interest" that is Willy's more characteristic response. He will help Willy with a job or with money, but he will not tell him what to do: he expects Willy, like Bernard, to make his own choice. Having subordinated sentiment to business efficiency all his life, Charley can allow his feelings to come through at Willy's funeral, and his final speech, "Nobody dast blame this man . . . ," though it is not the moral of the play, ought to have made unnecessary Miller's prefatory disavowal of any intended arraignment of big business.[6]

This tacit acceptance of business as long as it is kept distinct from sentiment is not a noticeably Marxist position. Yet Miller does not seem to intend a criticism of Howard for dismissing Willy ("When a man gets old you fire him, you have to, he can't do the work"):[7] but he contrives that dismissal so as to show Howard in as un-business-like a light as possible. The way in which Lawrence Newman is fired in *Focus*, on far more slender grounds, makes a marked contrast to this scene. Newman is being efficiently sacrificed to business efficiency where Willy, himself a bungler, is being dismissed by a man no better than himself. To this extent we sympathise with Willy's dilemma, but our respect is not given to either party, and the dramatic impact of this scene, properly played, ought to be one of inevitability—neither has any real alternative—and of littleness—neither is himself big enough to see the other, or to transcend his own sentimentality. Even Willy's eulogy of old Dave Singleman, who "was eighty-four years old, and he'd drummed merchandise in thirty-one states," and who "died the death of a salesman," has to be seen, for all its subdued eloquence, in this light. Strategically placed in this key scene, it constitutes a criticism of Willy in its garrulous irrelevance to this situation, and at the same time it is a condemnation of Howard for his failure to grasp its significance for Willy. Yet how little even this really means to Willy is ironically underlined in the next scene, when, tempted by Ben's offer of Alaskan wealth, he needs to be reminded of it by Linda:

BEN: What are you building? Lay your hand on it. Where is it?

WILLY [*hesitantly*]: That's true, Linda, there's nothing.

LINDA: Why? [*To Ben*] There's a man eighty-four years old. . . .

WILLY: That's right, Ben, that's right. When I look at
    that man I say, what is there to worry about?[8]

Ben's contemptuous "Bah!" is well-merited by the aura
that this has of a piece of family folk-lore, a germ of
Willy's self-deception to which Linda has been so re-
peatedly exposed that she has caught the infection worse
than he has.

Conflicting with the salesman-ideal of success in a
capitalist-commercial society, there is the pioneer-ideal
of success in the "great outdoors," represented for Willy
not only in the person of Ben but in the idealised race-
memory of the challenge of the frontier, embodied in his
father, who drove a waggon-team right across the country
selling flutes. There is also the popular image of success
through sporting prowess: Biff the hero of the football-
field is another dream whereby Willy seeks his own
identity. Neither of these is fully explored here; rather
are they introduced as stereotypes to which the popular
imagination always responds. Miller is very careful to
insist on all these sets of ideals as *Willy's*. He deliberately
provides no external documentation of Willy's memories
of his own earlier success as a salesman. We hear of it
only from Willy himself and, with less conviction, from
Linda; Howard disputes it and Charley never offers any
corroborative evidence. Similarly even the image of his
waggon-driving father is something second-hand, not
part of his own memory, but something he has been
told of by Ben, who himself is not a character, but a
creation of Willy's fancy. The title for the play was first
to have been *The Inside of his Head*,[9] and this in itself is
an admission that this is not tragedy in the usual sense
of the word, for tragedy postulates some external criteria,
which this conception deliberately precludes. It has been
often pointed out, too, that tragedy requires of its hero a
final recognition, of which, by his very nature, as well
as by the nature of the play, Willy Loman is incapable.

E

Tragedy implies values; and to the repeated complaint that Willy has no values, Miller has replied in these terms:[10]

The trouble with Willy Loman is that he has tremendously powerful ideals. We're not accustomed to speaking of ideals in his terms; but, if Willy Loman, for instance, had not had a very profound sense that his life as lived had left him hollow, he would have died contentedly polishing his car on some Sunday afternoon at a ripe old age. The fact is he has values. The fact that they cannot be realized is what is driving him mad—just as, unfortunately, it's driving a lot of other people mad. The truly valueless man, a man without ideals, is always perfectly at home anywhere.

Later in the same broadcast, however, Miller defined his aim in the play as being

to set forth what happens when a man does not have a grip on the forces of life and has no sense of *values which will lead him to that kind of a grip*.[11]

The two statements are not, as some critics argue, contradictory. They are in fact reconciled by Biff's epitaph on his father: "He had the wrong dreams. All, all wrong."[12] Charley's reply (already mentioned) amounts to little more than a plea in mitigation: Willy *had* to dream. The only person who challenges Biff's verdict is Happy, who is by now thoroughly discredited, any way; and Willy's suicide itself implies some recognition, even though limited, of his wrong values.

The phrase Miller used in his broadcast—"a man without ideals is always perfectly at home anywhere"—taken in conjunction with another already quoted—"How may a man make of the outside world a home?"—is revelatory. To be at home in the world is Willy's greatest desire, and it is not an unworthy one, even though as the aspiration of a tragic hero it is unthinkable.

In some respects *Death of a Salesman* is more important to
its generation than if it had been the tragedy it is sometimes censured for not being. One of the best defences of
it was written eighteen years before the play itself by
Aldous Huxley in an essay called "Tragedy and the
Whole Truth." These quotations attempt to summarise
his argument:

> To make a tragedy the artist must isolate a single
> element out of the totality of human experience and
> use that exclusively as his material. Tragedy is some-
> thing that is separated out from the Whole Truth. . . .
> Hence its power to act quickly and intensely on our
> feelings. . . .
>   In recent times literature has become more and more
> acutely conscious of the Whole Truth. . . . To impose
> the kind of arbitrary limitations, which must be im-
> posed by anyone who wants to write a tragedy, has
> become more and more difficult—is now indeed, for
> those who are at all sensitive to contemporaneity,
> almost impossible. This does not mean, of course, that
> the modern writer must confine himself to a merely
> naturalistic manner. One can imply the existence of
> the Whole Truth without laboriously cataloguing
> every object within sight. . . . Of all the important
> works of contemporary literature not one is a pure
> tragedy. There is no contemporary writer of signifi-
> cance who does not prefer to state or imply the Whole
> Truth.[13]

Miller, who is conceded to be "sensitive to contem-
poraneity" even by those to whom this is a term of abuse,
seems to me to have created something which in these
terms is not so much a tragedy as an exploration of the
Whole Truth (Huxley means the whole truth of a
situation, not the exhaustive exposition of a single
character). The final words of this essay may perhaps
close that particular debate:

There is no reason, after all, why the two kinds of literature . . . should not exist simultaneously, each in its separate sphere. The human spirit has need of both.

This chimes with an observation made by Miller in a letter in 1949:

However, it is obvious that I write out of life as I know it, rather than construct plays out of a theatrical imagination, as it were. The remembered thing about "Salesman" is really the basic situation in which these people find themselves—a situation which I have seen repeated throughout my life.[14]

That this was how audiences received the play is amusingly attested by Miller's own anecdotes on the correspondence he received about it,[15] and it is in this sense that it is a social drama of our times, but to say this is not to accept the frequently-encountered view that Willy is a modern Everyman. As Miller himself remarked with understandable brusqueness in the broadcast discussion:

Well, it's obvious that Willy Loman can't be an average American man, at least from one point of view; he kills himself.[16]

Miller has observed for himself the truth that Thoreau enunciated at the beginning of *Walden*: "The mass of men lead lives of quiet desperation." To this extent only is Willy Everyman. Before we apply to him Thornton Wilder's words, already quoted—"we see one of ourselves fighting, struggling and finally fainting in this inescapable American situation"—we ought to remember not only Miller's own comment but also the continuation of the Thoreau passage with which Miller seems in complete identity:

What is called resignation is confirmed desperation. . . . But it is a characteristic of wisdom not to do desperate things.

I have already suggested affinities between this play and *The Lonely Crowd*. Restated in Riesman's terms, it is the story of an "inner-directed" man whose efforts to "adjust" to an "other-directed" society result in *"anomie"* and the complete disintegration of personality. This, Riesman insists, is not only the undesirable, but also the atypical, response to the pressures of conformity. Willy's dilemma, that is, may be a common one, but Miller's (and the play's) attitude to it is neither as hopeless nor as unwisely desperate as Willy's.

What, then, ought Willy to do? The logic of all Miller's earlier writing, as well as of this play, rejects the notion of blinkered conformity as firmly as that of pig-headed resistance for its own sake; Miller's ideal, like Riesman's, is autonomy. How can Willy achieve it?

I am going to argue that he should fight the organization. But not self-destructively. . . . If he chafes at the pressures of his particular organization, either he must succumb, resist them, try to change them, or move to yet another organization.

Every decision he faces on the problem of the individual versus authority is something of a dilemma. It is not a case of whether he should fight against black tyranny or blaze a new trail against patent stupidity. That would be easy—intellectually, at least. The real issue is far more subtle. For it is not the evils of organization life that puzzle him, *but its very beneficence*. He is imprisoned in brotherhood. Because his area of manœuvre seems so small and because the trapping so mundane, his fight lacks the heroic cast, but it is for all this as tough a fight as ever his predecessors had to fight.

These are the words of William H. Whyte in *The Organization Man*.[17] They are not quoted to represent this as a play written to illustrate a thesis, but because the way in which the play's theme lends itself to restatement in so many different sets of terms is indicative of its density and of its centrality, its relevance to its society.

Nor is it only the sociologists who can interpret it. Within eight months of its opening on Broadway a neuro-psychiatrist had published an encomium of it as

visualized psychoanalytic interpretation woven into reality . . . [a] masterful exposition of the unconscious motivations in our lives. It is one of the most concentrated expressions of aggression and pity ever to be put on the stage.[18]

By some of the details of the argument the layman may be unconvinced (the play as "an irrational Oedipal blood-bath," the dinner to which Willy is invited as a totem-feast in which "the sons recognise the father's authority and sexual rights," and Willy's departure to the cloakroom as "castration-panic"), but its emphasis on the importance of the hallucinatory memory-sequences recognises one of the play's original contributions to dramatic structure:

The past, as in hallucination, comes back to him; not chronologically as in "flash-back", but *dynamically with the inner logic of his erupting volcanic unconscious*. In psychiatry we call this "the return of the repressed", when a mind breaks under the invasion of primitive impulses no longer capable of compromise with reality.

The interweaving of past and present in this play succeeds, of course, because of the organic relevance of the remembered episode to Willy's present situation. However unfamiliar Miller may claim to have been with Freudian psychology, he has certainly developed the motivating "inside-of-his-head" idea so smoothly and unobtrusively as to give the play a dramatic coherence more pleasing and more compulsive than his earlier more conventionally well-made plays had had.

He is particularly skilful in assimilating to it the realis-

tic techniques that had characterised his earlier works
and in revitalising them in the process. The shifts of
Willy's consciousness shuttling on a loom of memory
demand the maximum fluidity of movement, the minimum of scenery. There was no possibility of bringing
Willy's Chevrolet on to the stage for a polishing, even if
Miller had been inclined to repeat the errors of *The Man
who had all the Luck*. The alternative of dispensing with
scenery altogether had the precedent of *Our Town* to
commend it, but Thornton Wilder's evocation of a New
England town on the stage with the aid of a few chairs
and a loquacious stage-manager had succeeded only
because Grover's Corner was Everytown and did not
need localising. Willy Loman's house, with the mortgage
nearly repaid, is not as universal as it seems at first. In
one light it illustrates the problems of a property-owning
society, and it is not irrelevant again to recall Thoreau,
in the opening chapter of *Walden*, computing the average
income of a wage-earner and calculating that

> even if he is not encumbered with a family . . . he must
> have spent more than half his life commonly before *his*
> wigwam will be earned. . . . It may be guessed that I
> reduce almost the whole advantage of holding this
> superfluous property as a fund in store against the
> future, so far as the individual is concerned, mainly to
> the defraying of funeral expenses.

Thoreau proceeds to draw a typically dual moral that is
equally applicable to this play: "But perhaps a man is
not required to bury himself." Willy buries himself—
and this is surely Miller's point—in more ways than one,
and he need not go to a Thoreauvian extreme of pro-
perty renunciation to avoid this. The problem of material
property-ownership makes Willy's house as much of a
character in the play as the elms and the farmhouse had
been in Eugene O'Neill's *Desire under the Elms* in 1924.
Wisely Miller adapted to his own ends that stage-set of

the house in cross-section which has become so familiar in the American theatre that Kenneth Tynan could joke, a few years ago, that modern American drama "takes place either in a transparent doll's house with a porch (the porch is obligatory) or in the past; or both."

When Roderick Usher fell to the ground dead in the embrace of his resurrected sister and the narrator fled aghast—as well he might—he paused in the storm and, looking back, saw a fissure develop in the wall which opened to expose the interior of the doomed House of Usher as the whole edifice collapsed. In a poem of 1876 Browning describes the spectacle of a house ravaged by an earthquake:

> The whole of the frontage shaven sheer,
> The inside gaped.

The curious onlookers comment on this unexpected glimpse of the occupants' domestic arrangements:

> You see, it is proved, what the neighbours guessed:
> His wife and himself had separate rooms!

Browning's is the obvious Victorian moral:

> Friends, the goodman of the house at least
> Kept house to himself till the earthquake came:
> 'Tis the fall of its frontage permits you feast
> On the inside arrangements you praise or blame.

The cataclysms that cause the fall of the frontage of the houses of Eugene O'Neill's Ephraim Cabot and Ezra Mannon, of Tennessee Williams's Amanda Wingfield and Stanley Kowalski, and of Miller's Willy Loman, are psychological rather than meteorological, and have more in common with Poe than with Browning, but it is exactly that sense of disrupted privacy that is the keynote of this family drama. The "exploded" house set is integral to the impression at which all these plays aim, for not only does it mirror the family combustion that has come more and more to dominate the American theatre, but it is peculiarly suited to their dramatic idiom. Its stylised unnaturalness reminds us that we are in a theatre— we can see actions happening simultaneously, and often quite independently, in two places—while its revelatory intimacy ensures our engagement in the action. We can be, to adapt a phrase of Scott Fitzgerald's, "within and without simultaneously."

In the theatre Willy Loman's house is dwarfed by the omnipresence of the towering apartment houses all round it which, like O'Neill's elms, give the set a visual equivalent to the terrible claustrophobia of the play's theme. In a burst of misplaced agrarian escapism Willy goes out with a flashlight to set the seeds that he has some-how never found time to plant before. On a bare stage this might seem insufferably allegorical: with the setting Miller demands, this consideration is overwhelmed by the painful grotesqueness of the situation. Nothing brings out more sharply the pathetic ineffectualness and be-wilderment and littleness of the man than this scene, and the setting gives an added dimension to his otherwise petulant explosion:

Where the hell is that seed? You can't see nothing out here. They boxed in the whole goddam neighbor-hood.[19]

Leo Marx once analysed Melville's short story "Bartleby the Scrivener" under the suggestive title of "Melville's Parable of the Walls."[20] Emphasising the importance of the walls that enclose the unfortunate Bartleby and that contribute to his claustrophobic sense of "*anomie*," Marx rightly sees them as man-made and as symbolising the pressures on the individual of a man-made society. His summing-up applies, *mutatis mutandis*, to Loman as Miller sees him:

True, the society has been indifferent to Bartleby's

needs and aspirations . . . it has impaired his vision by forcing him to work in the shadow of its walls. Certainly society shares the responsibility for Bartleby's fate. But Melville will not go all the way with those who find in the guilt of society an excuse for [Bartleby's] every hallucination. To understand what led to Bartleby's behavior is not to condone it. Melville refuses to ignore the painful fact that even if society shares the blame for Bartleby's delusion, it was nevertheless a delusion. What ultimately killed [him] was not the walls themselves but the fact that he confused the walls built by men with the wall of human mortality.

That the stage walls by which the seed-planting Willy is boxed in are man-built of lath and canvas gives added irony to Miller's point. The walls to which Willy is a prisoner are less tangible than any of brick and stone, and yet by keeping us visually aware of those physical walls Miller simultaneously suggests the metaphysical walls as well. As the action of the play, taking place in Willy's mind, with effortless fluidity breaks through the walls of the stage house, the strength of the walls of his neurosis is accentuated. In the same way, in *Focus*, Lawrence Newman (whose place of work, like Bartleby's, is the Wall Street district) had sat in a glass-walled private office, a prisoner to inner terrors of which the transparent walls make him and us the more conscious.

It is, in short, a mistake to apply too strictly to *Death of a Salesman* the standards of realism by which the earlier plays ask to be judged. That we are never told the nature of the merchandise Willy sells or the surnames of any of the characters other than the Lomans is not a failure of the realistic method. Miller's own answer, "When asked what Willy was selling. . . . I could only reply, 'Himself' "[21]—is fair enough; these details are not necessary to a play that is nearer to expressionism than to realism. Eric Bentley asks:

Are the sons of Willy *seen* with the eye or just constructed from the *idea* that the present generation is
"lost"? Is Uncle Charlie [*sic*] of Alaska more than a
sentimental motif? Is Willy's marriage *there* for us to
inspect and understand down to its depths?[22]

To each of these questions the answer is that these things
are seen subjectively and developed only as far as Willy
himself is capable of taking them. Only twice does Miller
attempt to provide a brief external commentary, and to
have used any character in a role comparable to that of
Alfieri in *A View from the Bridge* would falsify the whole
play: we must see Willy's story as Willy sees it. This is
not, however, to encourage the reader to identify himself
with Willy or with any other character. Again, as with
Focus—and the parallels between the two could be
readily multiplied—the technique seems rather to be one
of "estrangement,"[23] to the extent that the author concentrates on the diversity of forces at work and wants his
audience to retain the capacity for objective judgment
rather than for emotional identification. At the same time
it has an expressionistic aspect in its concern with the
external world as perceived by the mind of the dreamer,
although it does not carry the distortion and fragmenta-
tion of that image to the lengths usually associated with
expressionism. This mixture of methods does not work
out completely successfully in the theatre, for a confusion
of response is almost inevitable. That it should have been
attempted at all is evidence of a theatrical adventurous-
ness that is itself a sign of health.

Its appeal to the ordinary theatre-goer on both sides of
the Atlantic is also a measure of Miller's success, even
though some of its admirers may tend to sentimentalise it.
Willy himself is a sentimentalist, particularly where the
past is concerned, but the sentimentality that is in that
respect a necessary element might have been a little more
effectively distanced, especially in the "Requiem." The

problem here is Linda. With none of the pathetic obsessions of Kate Keller and without the streak of un-
reasoning malice that Kate exhibits toward Ann, Linda
is just too good for Willy and thus too good for the play.
I do not mean that Linda is idealised: she is the most
decently moral member of the family, but her devotion
and loyalty to Willy are slightly over-emphasised and
over-articulated. In the "Requiem" it is her emotion
more than its cause to which we respond, because she is
herself confused about its cause. The Willy for whom she
weeps is not worth her tears for what he is so much as
for what he might have been, and although our vicarious
experience of sadness is a normal enough response to
another's bereavement, in this case it is obscuring for us
the perspective that the play should have sustained.
Linda's tears are for humanity: Biff is talking about an
individual, Happy is striking an attitude, while Charley
is extemporising on an idea. All are characteristic
reactions to the situation, and their very diversity is in
keeping with the sense of multiplicity that the play has
established. The difficulty is that an audience, instinc-
tively expecting a summing-up, fastens on the dominant
note, which is Linda's grief, and identifies itself with it.
The fault is not entirely Miller's, although in a moment of
self-criticism he confessed "My weakness is that I can create
pathos at will. It is one of the easiest things to do."[24]

It is also in part the outcome of his moral earnestness,
for earlier in the play he has used Linda as a mouthpiece
with a lack of subtlety that has often been commented
on (though sometimes exaggerated). This occurs at a
culminating point of Act I, and, being the one scene in
that Act which does not take place inside Willy's head,
gains an added air of objective reality. The whole scene
ought to be judged in its context, but one part of one
speech insists on isolating itself:

I don't say he's a great man. Willy Loman never

made a lot of money. His name was never in the paper. He's not the finest character that ever lived. But he's a human being, and a terrible thing is happening to him. So attention must be paid. He's not to be allowed to fall into his grave like an old dog. Attention, attention must be finally paid to such a person.[25]

The "attention" that she demands for him is out of proportion to the situation; it seems to be an attention more penetrating, more far-reaching, than can reasonably be expected of his sons (from whom, anyway, she is really demanding sympathetic understanding, not attention). Mary McCarthy comments on "the shrill, singsong voice of the mother":

She is really admonishing the audience that Willy is, as she says, "a human being." But that is just it; he is a Human Being without being anyone, a sort of suffering Statistic. The mother's voice raised in the old melancholy Jewish rhythms ("Attention must be paid" is not a normal American locution; nor is "finally", placed where it is; nor is "such a person" used as she uses it) seems to have been summoned from some other play that was about particular people.[26]

The implication that this would have been a better play had Miller rooted it more firmly in a Jewish milieu makes an attractive hypothesis, especially in the light of the success of Bernard Kops and Arnold Wesker more recently in this country. Miss McCarthy argues that Willy "could not be Jewish because he had to be American." Miller had a better reason than this for not stressing the Jewish element. The racial intermixture of the United States, in spite of the popular "melting-pot" image, has the paradoxical effect of often heightening racial consciousness. A markedly Jewish Willy Loman might have made the play seem an attack on covert anti-Semitism in American business, whereas by making Willy ethnically neutral Miller emphasises his point that Willy's trouble is that he is Willy in a particular society, not that he is a Jew, or a salesman, or a representative of any other group. In this one speech he is being presented as, in Miss McCarthy's words:

> a subject for the editorial page, which could take note of his working conditions, ask for unemployment benefits and old-age care for him, call "attention", in short, to the problem of the salesman in the Welfare State.

But Linda's speech throws into too high a relief something which is only one part—and that not the main—of a play more complex than it seems.

Speaking of *Our Town* Miller once remarked:

> I think that had Wilder drawn his characters with a deeper configuration of detail and with a more remorseless quest for private motive and self-interest, for instance, the story as it stands now would have appeared oversentimental and sweet. I think that if the play tested its own theme more remorselessly, the world it creates of a timeless family and a rhythm of existence beyond the disturbance of social wracks would not remain unshaken.[27]

This more remorseless testing of the theme is what *Death of a Salesman* attempts, and the sentimentality that Linda brings to it really comes from the "timeless family" and the "rhythm of existence" of *Our Town*. Linda is the one character in this play who ought to have been developed more fully because of her importance in the two scenes that do not take place inside Willy's head. As it is, she is too much "The Mother" and not enough an individualised Linda Loman.

Miller's comment on *Our Town* is offered in amplification of this proposition:

Every form, every style, pays its price for its special advantages. The price paid by *Our Town* is psychological characterization forfeited in the cause of the symbol.

It might be said that the price paid by *Death of a Salesman* is that the expectation of the symbol distracts the audience's attention from the psychological characterisation. American literature and literary criticism seem to have become preoccupied to the point of obsession with symbols and symbolism, but one would have been tempted in any case to think of Willy as a symbol of the little man. Perhaps the structure of the play does not make clear early enough the subjective angle from which Willy is being viewed; it begins so much like a realistic play that we have come to accept it as such before the first memory-sequence occurs, and we are not quick enough to see it as "the inside of his head." A more skilful use of language might have helped here. One reason why Linda focuses our attention is that she is the most articulate member of the household, so that some of her speeches stand out like the giant cacti in the Arizona desert of the surrounding dialogue. Had Willy's language approximated less successfully to the flatness of daily conversation, we might more readily have realised that we are to see the play through his eyes rather than through hers, but it would be difficult to make him more articulate without radically changing his character.

Mary McCarthy, while noting points of resemblance between Willy and King Lear, insists on two important distinctions between them. First, "No one could write an editorial calling attention to the case of King Lear"; second, and more important,

Lear, however, has the gift of language, which is not just a class-endowment, for the Fool has it too. This gift of language is what makes him human and not just "a human being".

Other critics smugly apply to Miller himself the remark that he made, probably with O'Neill in mind:

> We have had more than one extraordinary dramatist who was a cripple as a writer, and this is lamentable but not ruinous.[28]

The objections are not wholly fair, for some gift of language is apparent in Miller's acute ear for the banalities and inadequacies of daily conversation and for the rhythms of everyday speech. Miller could probably write the American equivalent of a Harold Pinter play—could, but would not want to, because, rightly or wrongly, he would not accept the implication that this is as far as most people can go in their use of language. At the same time his standards in this play, dictated by the theme, the situations and the characters themselves, are realistic. If in *All my Sons* the characteristic idiom is the unanswered question, in *Death of a Salesman* it is the cliché worn so smooth as to limit communication to the superficial and the unimportant. Up to this point in his development as a dramatist Miller has become progressively less hopeful about the possibilities of communication at a deeper level, but this marks the bottom of the curve on the graph and in the succeeding plays it climbs steadily upward, until eventually he formulates his practice into a theory. In the interim, the most that *Death of a Salesman* justifies our asking for is a suspension of judgment, coupled with the recognition of the dialogue's general fidelity to daily usage and of the fact that the more elevated language of tragedy would not be appropriate to a play that is not a tragedy any way.

REFERENCES

1. *Theatre Arts*, Nov. 1949, p. 13.
2. XVI (Jun. 1949), pp. 631–5. Passages quoted are from p. 633.
3. Quoted in *Best Plays 1948–9*, p. 53.
4. *C.P.*, p. 193.
5. *C.P.*, p. 191.
6. *C.P.*, pp. 221, 31, 37.
7. *C.P.*, p. 31.
8. *C.P.*, p. 184.
9. *C.P.*, p. 23.
10. The broadcast, originally transmitted from the University of Minnesota radio station, was published in revised form in *The Tulane Drama Review*, II (May 1958), pp. 63–69. The passage quoted is from p. 66 and should be compared with the exactly parallel passage at the foot of *C.P.*, p. 34.
11. *Op. cit.* p. 68: my italics.
12. *C.P.*, p. 221.
13. *Music at Night*, 1931. Penguin edn., Harmonds-worth 1955, pp. 14–15, 17.
14. Quoted in *Best Plays 1948–9*, pp. 53–4.
15. *C.P.*, pp. 27–8.
16. *The Tulane Drama Review*, II (May 1958), p. 66.
17. Pelican edn., Harmonds-worth 1960, pp. 16–17. The book was first published in New York in 1956.
18. Daniel E. Schneider, "Play of Dreams," in *Theatre Arts*, Oct. 1949, pp. 18–21.
19. *C.P.*, p. 213.
20. In *The Sewanee Review*, Oct. 1953.
21. *C.P.*, p. 28.
22. See above, n. 1.
23. Cp. above, p. 19.
24. *Theatre Arts*, Oct. 1953, p. 34.
25. *C.P.*, p. 162.
26. Mary McCarthy, *Sights and Spectacles 1937–1958*, London 1959, pp. xxiv–xxv.
27. "F.M.D.", p. 39.
28. *C.P.*, p. 8.

F

CHAPTER V

THE DEVIL IN SALEM

The witch-hunts that took place in Salem in 1692 were in the minds of many people two hundred and sixty years later. At least two other plays on the subject had reached the stage before *The Crucible* opened on Broadway on 22 January 1953. One of them, Florence Stevenson's *Child's Play*, had been performed at Oklahoma Civic Playhouse in the previous November and at Swarthmore Little Theatre in December, as well as winning the Frederick Warde prize at the Theater-Americana in California.[1] The other, by Louis O. Coxe (who had dramatised *Billy Budd* for Broadway presentation), was called *The Witchfinders*, and I remember seeing it in a studio-theatre production at the University of Minnesota at about the same time: the coincidental similarity of its subject-matter to that of *The Crucible* deterred Coxe from taking it further, but in other circumstances it would probably have done well. One of the factors behind this revival of interest was no doubt the appearance in 1949 of Marion L. Starkey's *The Devil in Massachusetts*, a very readable investigation into the whole issue from the psychological as well as from the historical standpoint, which had made a detailed account of the happenings and the trials more accessible than ever before. In the Introduction the author leaves us in no doubt as to one part of her purpose, telling us that

the story of 1692 is of far more than antiquarian interest; it is an allegory of our times. One would like to believe that leaders of the modern world can in the end deal with delusion as sanely and courageously as the men of old Massachusetts dealt with theirs.[2]

This is a recognisably twentieth-century attitude to the story, for when Hawthorne had written *The House of the Seven Gables* the witch-hunt had been regarded as an iniquity to be expiated by the later generations to whom Maule's curse descended, rather than as a triumph for the American way of life. But this is to put it unfairly, for, if Hawthorne and his contemporaries saw it primarily as an illustration of "man's inhumanity to man," and a matter of sin and personal guilt, they did not have our reasons for looking at it in the wider social context that leads Marion Starkey to speak of the "ideological intensities which rent its age no less than they do ours," and to remind us that:

> Only twenty witches were executed, a microscopic number compared to . . . the millions who have died in the species of witch-hunts peculiar to our own rational, scientific times.[3]

By the autumn of 1952 these words had been given greater immediacy by the mounting fury of the latest species of witch-hunt being conducted by Senator Joseph McCarthy as a Congressional investigation into un-American activities.

Here was an important subject ready to hand for an able dramatist to exploit, and Miller was the obvious man to tackle it. His background of Depression-engendered liberalism, his passionate belief in social responsibility, and his proven ability to handle themes of guilt and punishment, all qualified him for it. Indeed, he had almost inevitably been moving towards it for longer than he had realised. We hardly need his specific assurance that he "had known of the Salem witch hunt for many years before 'McCarthyism' had arrived"; more illuminating is his passing reference to two of his earliest "desk-drawer" plays:

... a play about two brothers caught on either side of radicalism in a university, then a play about a psychologist's dilemma in a prison where the sane were inexorably moving over to join the mad.[4]

These sound like modern versions of two of the themes of *The Crucible*, and the former might well have been an interesting variant of the two-brother pattern that I traced in an earlier chapter, but I doubt whether a revision of either play would have been as effective a way of dramatising the problems of 1952 as *The Crucible*. The objection that Salem does not present a sufficiently precise parallel, because "whereas witchcraft was pure delusion, subversion is a reality, no matter how unwisely or intemperately it may be combatted,"[5] ignores Miller's implication that, where evidence is only circumstantial, the dividing line between delusion and reality is so difficult to draw that the utmost caution is essential.

It also confuses the main issue of Miller's play which is much wider than this admits. He had been moving towards it in adapting *An Enemy of the People*, which had attracted him because it dealt with

... the central theme of our social life today. Simply, it is the question of whether the democratic guarantees protecting political minorities ought to be set aside in time of crisis. More personally, it is the question of whether one's vision of the truth ought to be a source of guilt at a time when the mass of men condemn it as a dangerous and devilish lie. It is an enduring theme ... because there never was, nor will there ever be, an organized society able to countenance calmly the individual who insists that he is right while the vast majority is absolutely wrong.[6]

By treating this problem in a seventeenth- rather than in a twentieth-century context, Miller sacrifices the questionable advantage of extreme topicality for the greater gain of perspective. He is insisting on this as a perennial American problem, not merely a present-day one. The terms in which he defines his anxiety reminds us of this in yet another way:

> I saw accepted the notion that conscience was no longer a private matter but one of state administration. I saw men handing conscience to other men and thanking other men for the opportunity of doing so.[7]

This is a modern restatement of Thoreau's central question in *On the Duty of Civil Disobedience*: "Must the citizen ever for a moment, or in the least degree, resign his conscience to the legislator?" (The frequent analogies adduced between Miller and Thoreau are intended to relate Miller to his predecessor in spirit only and not to imply direct influence.) It follows that, while fully accepting Miller's statement that he could not have written the play at any other time, I am disinclined to treat it narrowly as a tract against McCarthyism. Miller's own position on that issue is better discussed biographically, and the play itself is much more interesting than the sordid chapter of career-politics that occasioned it.

To begin with, it is of interest as an historical play, by which I mean something more than a mere costume-drama. Miller provides a note on its historical accuracy which indicates the care he has taken over it,[8] and reference to Marion Starkey's account or to the primary sources will quickly substantiate this. (As many as possible of the original documents bearing on the events and the trials were collated in a three-volume typescript in Essex County in 1938; that this was a Works Progress Administration project provides yet another instance of the influence—unexpected, belated, and indirect this time—of the Depression on Miller's work.) To document this would be tedious: sufficient, perhaps, to mention as an example the book written in 1697 by John Hale: *A*

Modest Inquiry into the Nature of Witchcraft.[9] There is an obvious identity between Miller's character in *The Crucible* and the man whose ambivalent attitude to the whole proceedings may be seen from the following extracts:

> I observed in the prosecution of these affairs, that there was in the Justices, Judges and others concerned, a conscientious endeavour to do the thing that was right.

Nevertheless, he is not easy in his own conscience, though what he questions is legal procedure rather than witchcraft itself:

> We may hence see ground to fear that there hath been a great deal of innocent blood shed in the Christian World, by proceeding upon unsafe principles, in condemning persons for Malefick Witchcraft.

There is a similar reservation in his recognition of the need for restitution to some (not, apparently, to all) of the victims:

> I would humbly propose whether it be not expedient, that some what more should be publickly done than yet hath, for clearing the good name and reputation of some that have suffered upon this account.

Hale is prepared to admit that he and his colleagues may have made mistakes in an excess of zeal; he is still convinced that witchcraft may exist and that vigilance must be maintained:

> Seeing we have been too hard against supposed Malefick Witchcraft, let us take heed we do not on the contrary become too favourable to divining Witchcraft [*sc.* fortune-telling.]

The note of uncertainty, of suspended judgment, that these quotations reveal is very close to the keynote of this play, which I find in the constant recurrence, on the lips

of many different characters, of the phrase "I think."
Much of the play could be summarised in Yeats's lines:

> The best lack all conviction, while the worst
> Are full of passionate intensity.

It is not so much a story of two ideologies in conflict as a
story of conscientious endeavour in an uncertain world.
This emerges with particular force and clarity in Act II,
in, for example, such exchanges as this, in which Elizabeth Proctor tells her husband what she has heard from
Mary Warren:

ELIZABETH: The Deputy Governor promise hangin' if
   they'll not confess, John. The town's gone wild, I
   think. She speak of Abigail, and I thought she were
   a saint, to hear her. . . .
PROCTOR: Oh, it is a black mischief.
ELIZABETH: I think you must go to Salem, John. I
   think so. You must tell them it is a fraud.[10]

Joe Keller had asked in vain for guidance: no one could
give it to him. Willy Loman's bewilderment at Charley,
who had never told his son what to do, is the bewilderment of the man who has confidently inculcated in his
own sons a complete set of values that have turned out to
be wrong (just as Ben's advice to Biff, "Never fight fair
with a stranger, boy," is, in its context, implicitly criticised).[11] In *The Crucible* the wiser characters do not pre-
sume to dictate anyone's duty to him, for that would
be asking him to hand over his conscience. Moreover,
they themselves are too perplexed by the conflicting
implications of the issues to be dogmatic. Elizabeth's
quietly-delivered suggestions here are the thoughts of a
worried but honest mind spoken aloud for her husband's
benefit, and he replies in the same key: "I'll think on
it. . . . I think it is not easy to prove she's fraud, and the
town gone so silly." Far from indicating a limited
vocabulary, either of character or author, the repetition

of this formula "I think" is in fact a very skilfully-managed way of suggesting the scruples, the misgivings, and the conscientious earnestness which are all that these people can bring against the diabolic impetus of the witch-hunt. It is significant that Miller chose to dramatise the story of John Proctor, the plain farmer, rather than the equally well-documented story of George Burrough, the minister, who was also accused of witchcraft and hanged for it. Miller's invention of Proctor's earlier adultery with Abigail is not the outcome of a mercenary desire to add a spice of sensationalism to the play. It is a similar insistence on the human vulnerability of a man who is not a saint, not even an ordained minister fortified by a theological training, but just a decent man trying to understand and to translate into action the dictates of his conscience, trying to do, not what he *feels*, but what he *thinks*, is right.

In this concern with conscience, and in other respects, too, *The Crucible* seems to be the most Shavian of Miller's plays. This is apparent in an immediate, but not super-ficial, respect when we notice how the printed text of this play is accompanied by a lengthy prefatory comment on the background, and by a postscript tracing the subse-quent history of the characters; the dialogue of the open-ing scene, in particular, is also interrupted more than once for a Shavian elaboration on the theme, which is not in any sense a stage-direction. Miller had done something similar for a paperback edition of *Death of a Salesman* issued by Bantam Books in New York in 1951, but in the *Collected Plays* he reverts to the original text of this play. *The Crucible*, however, is a play for Puritans in Shaw's, as well as in the more historically literal, sense, and also has more in common with *St Joan* in particular than has been generally remarked. It is not just that each is a religious-historical play culminating in an impressive trial scene followed by martyrdom. In both the tension is further heightened by a dramatic *peripateia* in which the prisoner, having made a "confession" to escape death, suddenly realises the implications of it and recants by tearing the confession to pieces. The resemblance also extends to quite small incidents, as, for example, Proctor's conversation with his servant in Act II when he orders her to bed:

MARY WARREN: I'll not be ordered to bed no more, Mr. Proctor! I am eighteen and a woman, however single!

PROCTOR: Do you wish to sit up? Then sit up.

MARY WARREN: I wish to go to bed!

PROCTOR [in anger]: Good night, then![12]

In a similar way the Inquisitor, at Joan's trial, orders the English Chaplain, Stogumber, to sit down, and, when he refuses, replies, "If you will not sit, you must stand: that is all"; this is probably a more calculated move than Proctor's blunt directness, but it produces the same petulant compliance by the other person, for Stogumber immediately sits. It is of another aspect of Stogumber that we are reminded in the trial scene of *The Crucible* by the Reverend Parris, whose misplaced zeal makes him not only ridiculously quick to see insults to the dignity of the court in remarks that his betters are undisturbed by, but also makes him vindictive and severe in his questions to witnesses and in his fear lest any possible charge should be omitted.

Stogumber comes to mind yet again in Act IV, when Hale sees the consequences of his zeal. A more intelligent man than Stogumber, he is less abject, less hysterical, in his recognition of guilt, but his cry to Danforth—"There is blood on my head! Can you not see the blood on my head?"—is approaching hysteria; and his appeal to Elizabeth to persuade her husband to save his life by lying allows emotion to swamp principle: "Cleave to no faith when faith brings blood."[13] Like Stogumber, he has needed to see the suffering of others before he can

realise the implications of his own actions, and, like
Stogumber, his immediate inclination is to swing to the
other extreme. If we enquire why Miller does not humili-
ate Hale as Shaw humiliates the Chaplain, we are
brought to the heart of both plays. To play Stogumber
as a fool up to the burning of Joan and then to swing the
audience's sympathy to him by his breakdown at the
end of that scene is a temptation to any actor, but it
blurs Shaw's point. Stogumber's collapse must be more
grotesque than pathetic. This makes greater demands on
the actor, but Warwick's attitude to him and the per-
sistence of Stogumber's own chauvinistic narrowness are
clear indications of Shaw's intentions, just as are the
ineffectualness and silliness of Stogumber in the Epilogue.
Stogumber's importance in the trial scene is far in excess
of the comic relief that it is generally taken for: he is the
bigot, the fanatic, and, above all, the self-deceiver who
has allowed his principles to be overwhelmed by his
passions. All the other members of the court, as Shaw
emphasises in his Preface, were "far more self-disciplined
and conscientious . . . than any English judge ever
dreams of being in a political case in which his party
and class prejudices are involved"; all of them act
honestly, coolly, and in full accordance with their own
convictions. Shaw's contempt is reserved for Stogumber,
the one man who allows prejudice to blind him to his
real moral beliefs.

Now Miller starts out from a wholly different premise,
for which he claims the historical authority of his sources:

I do not think that either the record itself or the
numerous commentaries upon it reveal any mitigation
of the unrelieved, straightforward, and absolute dedication to evil displayed by the judges of these trials and
the prosecutors. After days of study it became quite
incredible how perfect they were in this respect.[14]

Hale, that is, like Stogumber, is the one exception, but in

the opposite direction: he is the only one in whom there is
any glimmer of hope, and as such he cannot be mocked
as Stogumber is, though Miller's knowledge of human
nature prevents him from sanctifying Hale's repentance.
Danforth, Hathorne, and Parris are worse than Shaw's
Chaplain: they are not only bigoted fanatics, but Miller
sees them as positively evil (which Shaw never suggests
Stogumber is), and he has said categorically that if he
were to re-write the play, he would accentuate this evil
still more.[15] He adds:

> I believe merely that, from whatever cause, a dedica-
> tion to evil, not mistaking it for good, but knowing
> it as evil and loving it as evil, is possible in human
> beings who appear agreeable and normal. I think now
> that one of the hidden weaknesses of our whole
> approach to dramatic psychology is our inability to
> face this fact—to conceive, in effect, of Iago.

In American literature, probably more than in any
other, there have always been influences at work to
minimise the fact of evil. At the extreme there is the
Emersonian Transcendentalism optimistically asserting
that "Good is positive. Evil is merely privative, not absolute: it is like cold, which is the privation of heat,"
and "There is no pure lie, no pure malignity in nature.
The entertainment of the proposition of depravity is the
last profligacy and profanation."[16] The Declaration of
Independence may be said to have made evil an un-
American activity, and although the buoyancy that
American literature acquires from this heritage of optimism is often invigorating, yet it can be a limitation. Its
writers have generally been quicker to recognise evils than
to recognise evil. Part of the superiority of Melville and
James over Hawthorne lies in their ability to conceive of
evil where he thinks only in terms of sin, and Faulkner's
superiority over many of his contemporaries is in part
attributable to his awareness of evil where they see psy-

chological maladjustment and environmental deprivation.

It is salutary, then, to find Miller enunciating this general belief in the need for literature to recognise evil, but it is a little disconcerting to find it in this specific context. The dedication to evil, of which he speaks, "not mistaking it for good, but *knowing it as evil* [my italics] and loving it as evil," may perhaps be imputed in this play—and we may disregard the sources in this discussion—to those characters who deliberately and cynically give false evidence, or incite others to do so, for their own personal gain or gratification. This means Thomas Putnam, with his greed for land, and Abigail, with her lust for Proctor. Putnam, however, is only a minor character, and Miller himself (as I shall shortly indicate) seems in two minds about the extent to which Abigail is evil or merely deluded. Evil can with much less certainty be imputed to the judges, who, hard and cruel as they may have been by our standards, and even culpably credulous, were trying, both in history and in the play, to judge in the light of evidence of an unprecedented nature. To make them more evil would be to destroy by distortion one of the virtues of the play in its present form. The very considerable dramatic power of *The Crucible* derives from its revelation of a mounting tide of evil gaining, in an entire society, an ascendancy quite disproportionate to the evil of any individual member of that society. What is so horrifying is to watch the testimony of honest men bouncing like an indiarubber ball off the high wall of disbelief that other men have built around themselves, not from ingrained evil, but from over-zealousness and a purblind confidence in their own judgment. What meaning has proof when men will believe only what they want to believe, and will interpret evidence only in the light of their own prejudice? To watch *The Crucible* is to be overwhelmed by the simple impotence of honest common sense against fanaticism that is getting out of control, and to be painfully reminded that there are situations in which sheer goodness ("mere unaided virtue," in Melville's ~~phrase about~~ Starbuck) is just not enough to counter such deviousness.

In this respect, too, it will remain a more important document of McCarthy's America than would a more partisan piece. The ugliness of that affair, which caused so much perplexed anxiety to friends of the United States, was not the megalomanic aspirations of a cynical demagogue, but the appalling ease with which his methods achieved results. So fast and so wide did the infection spread that it could only be visualised as a force of evil of which ordinary men and women were the unintentional agents and the unrecognising victims. In many ways its moral damage was more serious to those who accepted it than to those who fought against or were victimised by it, and this is what *The Crucible* so splendidly communicates. In the Introduction to the *Collected Plays*, Miller brings this out very movingly by his anecdotes of the investigations,[17] and then obscures it by his retrospective attribution of a greater evil to the individual judges of Salem. *The Crucible*, of course, was written before Miller's own clash with the Congressional Committee, and is in that respect less biased, perhaps, than the later Introduction. The real moral of the play is the very Shavian one that in the life of a society evil is occasioned less by deliberate villainy than by the abnegation of personal responsibility. That is why Elizabeth quietly rejects as "the Devil's argument" Hale's impassioned plea:

> Beware, Goody Proctor—cleave to no faith when faith brings blood. It is a mistaken law that leads you to sacrifice. Life, woman, life is God's most precious gift; no principle, however glorious, may justify the taking of it.[18]

Elizabeth, like St Joan, has learnt through suffering that "God's most precious gift" is not life at any price, but the life of spiritual freedom and moral integrity. Her simple reply to Hale substantiates a point I have already made: "I think that be the Devil's argument." She believes this, but she cannot prove it: "I cannot dispute with you, sir; I lack learning for it"; and again, as in *St Joan*, the learning of the scholars, the theologians, and the rulers is discredited, but not defeated, by the simple faith of a country woman.

The communication of this faith is Miller's best technical achievement in this play, for it depends very largely on his command of a new form of language specially adapted to the demands of his theme. Just as *St Joan* (to draw one final parallel) is the most poetic of Shaw's plays, so the language of *The Crucible* is heightened in exactly similar ways. However, where Shaw gives Joan a country dialect largely for anti-romantic and comic-realistic effect ("Where be Dauphin?" and "Thou art a rare noodle, Master"), the rustic-archaic speech of Miller's characters gives them such a natural eloquence and simple dignity that he does not need to abandon it as Shaw does in the more highly-charged situations but can (as my quotations will have shown) use it to good purpose throughout. It is simple and unpretentious, relying mainly on the use of unusual forms of the verb and on "Mister" as a form of address that becomes unexpectedly successful in its suggestion of an unsophisticated kind of antagonistic formality. Far from finding its quaintness disturbing in the theatre, I have been impressed by its self-controlled candour even on the lips of English actors, and it contributes significantly to the keynote of the play, which I have defined as one of conscientious endeavour in an uncertain world. There is a forthrightness about *The Crucible* that is well supported by its language as well as by its structural simplicity. Miller has commented:

I was drawn to this subject because the historical

moment seemed to give me the poetic right to create
people of higher self-awareness than the contemporary
scene affords. I had explored the subjective world in
Salesman and I wanted now to move closer to a conscious hero.[19]

He has thus taken one step towards the greater faith in
human nature that he defined in discussing "The
Misfits," and it is this that offsets and mitigates the power
of darkness that dominates so much of the action.

It is not Proctor's heroism that matters so much as his
consciousness:

> A point has to arrive where man sees what has hap-
> pened to him. I think *The Crucible* is not more realistic
> but more theatrical than *Death of a Salesman*.

Thus Miller himself, in an interview in October 1953, in
which he also spoke of himself as "trying to find a way, a
form, a method of depicting people who do think."[20] Six
months after the play's New York opening Miller made
some changes in the text, including the addition of a new
scene, and critics are reported to have found the new
version "more fluid, forceful and poetic." The changes
mainly affected Proctor's part, making it more lyrical in
Act II by the introduction of such lines as "Lilacs have a
purple smell. Lilac is the smell of nightfall, I think."[21]
Similarly, in Act IV, his final speech to his wife had originally consisted simply of the exhortation "Give them
no tear! Show a stony heart and sink them with it!"; the
revision made him answer Hale (whom he had previously
ignored) and expanded the speech as follows:

HALE: Man, you will hang! You cannot!
PROCTOR [*his eyes full of tears*]: I can. And there's your
first marvel, that I can. You have made your magic
now, for now I do think I see some shred of goodness in John Proctor. Not enough to weave a banner
with, but white enough to keep it from such dogs.

[Elizabeth, in a burst of terror, rushes to him and weeps against his hand.] Give them no tear! Tears pleasure them! Show honor now, show a stony heart and sink them with it![22]

It is not his heroism so much as his self-awareness that is increased by the change, just as his forthrightness had been emphasised by the introduction of the Cheever episode in Act III,[23] as well as by minor additions elsewhere.

A less happy addition was a short scene in a wood, which was inserted before the trial scene.[24] In it Proctor, on the eve of his wife's trial, meets Abigail to warn her of his intention to denounce her in court unless she abjures her denunciation of witches. Abigail, however, half-crazed with religious mania and with frustrated love for Proctor (of which she reminds him passionately) does not believe him:

PROCTOR: . . . and you will never cry witchery again, or I will make you famous for the whore you are!

ABIGAIL *[she grabs him]*: Never in this world! I know you, John—you are this moment singing secret Hallelujahs that your wife will hang!

PROCTOR *[throws her down]*: You mad, you murderous bitch!

ABIGAIL: . . . Fear naught. I will save you tomorrow. From yourself I will save you.

Obviously it is a powerful but quite superfluous scene, and Miller was wise to abandon it in subsequent editions. Its removal suggests, as I remarked earlier, that he is in two minds about Abigail, for in this scene her religiosity makes her more pathetically deluded than evil, so that the second thoughts which lead him to cut it out may be connected with the desire to accentuate the element of evil. In any case, the past relationship between Proctor and Abby has been clearly established in the first two

Acts; Proctor's eyes have been opened to her true nature
by the circumstances of his wife's arrest, after which he is
hardly likely to seek a secret interview with her alone (if
only for fear of being accused of interfering with a
witness); and his disclosure of his intentions detracts
from the dramatic power of the moment in Act III when
he confesses his adultery. By the end of Act II, our attention has been effectively directed to Proctor, and the
spotlight of the action is already narrowing into focus on
his eventual clash with the court, so that we are becoming
impatient of incidents that do not materially bear upon
that. Thus this wood scene is an embarrassment, as is
also the opening passage of Act IV, with Tituba and
Sarah Good, which could easily be dispensed with as a
distraction.

In general Miller is very skilful in his manipulation of
his large cast. The characters are neatly differentiated
and are all well utilised individually and corporately to
develop the sense of a community. The only exception
might be Francis Nurse, who is kept on the stage for a
considerable part of Act II and even more of Act III
with nothing to do; no exit is marked for him in Act II,
though he obviously leaves with Corey, and no cue for
his entrance is given in Act III, though he is in the room
when Danforth orders it to be cleared.[25] In the very
earliest version of the play Miller seems to have reverted
to the more extended manner of narration he was using
before *All my Sons*: an opening scene set in a forest had to
be abandoned because of the cost of building the set, but
it is unlikely to have done much that is not better done in
the final version by retrospective description. Something
of the old realism still survives in some of the detailed
settings and stage directions (at one point Danforth is
even directed to blow his nose).[26] Most interesting in this
respect is Miller's preoccupation with the source of light
in each scene. In Act I the sun streams through the leaded
panes of a narrow window; in Act III sunlight pours

G

through two high windows; in Act IV moonlight seeps through the bars of another high window. This may not be readily translatable into a lighting plot, but it shows how Miller sees the mood of the play—darkness and gloom penetrated by the single shaft of light cast by conscientiously dogged goodness. The revised version of July 1953, staged under Miller's own direction, "did away with all scenery, and had the action take place against drapes and a light-flooded cyclorama." The starkness of such a production would well suit the starkness of the play's theme, for it is a play that hovers on the brink of nihilism in a nightmare of lost innocence. "If Rebecca Nurse be tainted, then nothing's left to stop the whole green world from burning."[27] In simple phrases like this there is an eloquence of agony that makes this even more moving theatrically than *Death of a Salesman*, because there is no question of sentimentality. The Proctors' children, though mentioned, never appear. Our pity is demanded for an adult world run mad. When Proctor turns on Hale, the plain ordinariness of his language, lit by an unexpected simile, a rhetorical repetition, and an inversion of the normal order of two adjectives, is all that is needed to make it adequate to a situation that has already been brought almost unbearably close to us:

> Why do you never wonder if Parris be innocent, or Abigail? Is the accuser always holy now? Were they born this morning as clean as God's fingers? I'll tell you what's walking Salem—vengeance is walking Salem. We are what we always were in Salem, but now the little crazy children are jangling the keys of the kingdom, and common vengeance writes the law![28]

There are more kinds of poetry, and more ways of attacking McCarthyism, than one. Anything more high-flown would be out of place in this play which insists so relentlessly on the precariousness of the foothold of goodness in a world swept by a wind of evil blowing at hurricane force.

REFERENCES

1. *Theatre Arts*, Feb. 1953, p. 91.
2. Marion L. Starkey, *The Devil in Massachusetts*, New York 1949; London 1952, p. 11.
3. *Op. cit.*, p. 10.
4. *C.P.*, pp. 41, 14.
5. Quoted by Krutch, *American Drama since 1918*, N.Y. 1957, p. 325.
6. *E.P.*, pp. 8–9.
7. *C.P.*, p. 40.
8. *C.P.*, p. 224.
9. Published posthumously in Boston, 1702. Reprinted in *Narratives of the Witchcraft Cases*, ed. G. L. Burr, New York 1914. The quotations given are from this reprint, pp. 415, 425, 427, 431.
10. *C.P.*, p. 263.
11. *C.P.*, p. 158.
12. *C.P.*, p. 269.
13. *C.P.*, pp. 319, 320.
14. *C.P.*, pp. 42–3.
15. *C.P.*, pp. 43–4.
16. These quotations come respectively from ''The Divinity School Address'' and the essay ''New England Reformers.''
17. *C.P.*, pp. 39–40.
18. *C.P.*, p. 320.
19. *C.P.*, p. 44.
20. In *Theatre Arts*, Oct. 1953, pp. 33–4. This is also the source of information about production changes discussed in this chapter. It also printed the whole revised text of the play.
21. *C.P.*, p. 262.
22. *C.P.*, p. 328.
23. *C.P.*, p. 290. The whole of the dialogue from Cheever's first speech at the top of the page to the beginning of Danforth's 4 ll. from the bottom was introduced for the first time in the revision.
24. The play had originally been a two-act play, each act having two scenes. In the Acting Edition (1953) this new scene is called Act II, Sc. 1, so that the present Acts III and IV became Act II, Scs. 2 and 3 respectively. On the other hand, the *Theatre Arts* text of the play divides it into four acts and describes this scene, which it does not number, as a "sequence added to Act II" (*i.e.*, following immediately upon the arrest of Elizabeth).
25. In *C.P.*, he is ignored between p. 277 and p. 283, and in Act III he enters at p. 287, but between p. 288 and p. 311 he speaks only at pp. 292–3 and 304 (one line).
26. *C.P.*, p. 298.
27. *C.P.*, p. 277.
28. *C.P.*, p. 281.

CHAPTER VI

TWO NEW YORK PLAYS

The development of Miller's drama traced so far has been towards greater simplicity of form. Not since *The Man who had all the Luck* has he made any use of a sub-plot; not since *All my Sons* has there been any attempt at the artificial surprise of the delayed revelation. Form has varied from play to play, not out of a facile desire for novelty, but according to the dictates of the nature of each play. Language has become modestly richer and more varied, though remaining firmly rooted in daily speech. His view of life remains fundamentally serious (there is as yet no *Ah, Wilderness!* in the Miller canon, as there is in O'Neill), but it has developed and, in *The Crucible*, can conceive of and find room for a kind of heroism. And each play has broken new ground.

This is true of his latest pair of plays, *A Memory of two Mondays* and *A View from the Bridge*, produced as a double bill on Broadway in September 1955. The opening performance was unfortunate and unimpressive, as Miller himself admits,[1] the run was shorter than that of any of his plays since his first (if we except the Ibsen adaptation), and it was listed by *Variety* as a financial failure. Although *A View from the Bridge* was included in *The Best Plays of 1955–56*, neither of the two plays received any prizes, yet neither is markedly inferior to his other work.

A Memory of two Mondays is the more straightforward. A deeply-felt piece of autobiographical nostalgia, it is the most dated of all Miller's work: "so much so," he confesses wryly, "that many took it for granted it had been written a long time ago and exhumed."[2] This is not because, as Miller suggests, "the play speaks not of obsession but of rent and hunger and the need for a little poetry in life", but rather because, in doing so, it evokes so successfully the atmosphere of the nineteen-thirties. Nothing is more out of date than last week's newspaper, and the attitude, if not the form, of this play is imaginatively close to the idea of the "Living Newspaper" with which the Federal Theater Project had experimented. It is a commonplace that American literature of the past eighty years has had its roots more deeply in journalism than has, for example, English literature. The number of American writers from Twain, Howells, and Stephen Crane to Hemingway, Steinbeck, and Miller himself who have served an apprenticeship in journalism is indicative. Miller has more than once defined the duty of the dramatist as "to bring the news," and Mary McCarthy defines the novelist's responsibility in the same phrase. None of Miller's plays "brings the news" in a more literal sense than this one, and yet it does it without the obvious and tedious documentation of topical allusion. Beyond passing—and unobtrusive—references to Hitler and Roosevelt, it is more a matter of mood and atmosphere delicately conveyed. Miller expresses surprise "that it was seen as something utterly sad and hopeless as a comment on life," and tries to oppose to this the fact that the play shows Bert working his way out of "this endless, time-less, will-less environment," but this is a misleading argument. It is not Bert who stays in our mind so much as the company in which he moves, and what we remember of them is their aura of diminished hope. It is not "utterly sad," but it is what Miller calls it—"a pathetic comedy" or a documentary of the nineteen-thirties. Discretion or retrospect has eliminated the element of propaganda that would have been prominent had it been written at the time, and the pathetic is well kept in check by touches of humour, and also by a realistic grasp of human nature that goes beyond pathos. The personal ties that develop between people whose employment brings them together during working hours are shown with real insight: one-sided, trivial, facetious, and often irritated, yet in some ways deep and at times even agonising. The relationships between these characters are the most casual of any in Miller's plays and the play sets out to prove less than do the others, but, even while it insists on the transience and ultimate unsatisfactoriness of such relationships, it communicates an unusual sense of the warmth they may generate. Within its limited scope the character of Gus— bawdy, sentimental, irascible, irresponsible, yet generous, kind-hearted, and with his own sense of values and loyalty —is one of Miller's richest achievements, and the speech in which he traces his twenty-two years with the firm in terms of the car-models he has outlived is at once lifelike and in its own way poetic.[3] A comparison with the Gus of *The Man who had all the Luck* would provide a quick and convenient index of Miller's progress as a dramatist.

If in most respects this is a minor play, it is clearly a minor play by a major playwright who has learnt to co-ordinate all the constituent elements into a unified pattern. Thus the counterpoise of the two halves of the play, already suggested by the title, is worked out simply but effectively by a see-saw relationship between two of the characters. Tommy, the drunken clerk of the first part, becomes, by a tremendous effort of will, the triumphant teetotaller of the second, while Kenny, at first a poetry-spouting, likably rough Irish idealist, has by the second part begun the process of degeneration into a drunken lout, though with flashes of the old decency still surviving. There is no direct causal connexion between the changes that take place in the two men, they have no influence on each other, nor is there any significant interaction between them in the story. In the second part, however, we recognise a loss of vitality in both of them: the reformed Tommy has a priggish rectitude and hard-ness that are much less attractive than his earlier, if unregenerate, warmth; and the Kenneth who has turned to drink as an anodyne has lost the rugged spontaneity that he had at first. The passage of time is hinted at by these unobtrusive signs of ageing in all the characters in the second part. Realising that Tommy and Kenneth have lost some of their earlier attractiveness, we realise that the others have also calcified a little. The two Mondays are separated by the time it takes a young man, Bert, to earn enough money for his first year at college. It is through his memory that we see the warehouse, its occupants and the action of the play, and thus there is no formal division into scenes. The continuity of flow suggests the unity of Bert's experience, and if the time-gap is marked only by a short semi-lyrical exchange between Bert and Kenneth and a brief soliloquy, this is how Bert's memory sees it. With the exception of Tommy and Kenneth, it is not the characters who have changed so much as Bert, who has matured in his view of them.

Here again Miller is examining in his own way a theme that has had a peculiar fascination for the American writer. From Hawthorne's "My Kinsman, Major Molineux," via *Huckleberry Finn* to Salinger's *The Catcher in the Rye*, American fiction has always been challenged by the idea of growing up, by the situation of the adolescent caught between the millstones of childhood and adult life. It is a theme closely connected, of course, with the theme of initiation mentioned in my second chapter, and one that lends itself readily to the exploration of the impact of evil on the young mind. One aspect of *The Crucible* connects with this, and so, really, does the role of Chris in *All my Sons*, for I suspect that many readers, looking back on that play, share my surprise at the stage direction that describes him as thirty-two: one thinks of him as a good deal younger, surely, in his innocence. However, what gives *A Memory of two Mondays* its particular quality is the passivity of the role of the boy himself. Evil is not involved, and the play is more concerned with

initiation into an understanding of the lives of others
than with initiation into self-knowledge. Bert does nothing
to further such action as the play has: nothing is done
to him in any violent sense; he is exposed to experience
in a way that is at once lifelike and artistically satisfying
in a Chekhovian manner. This exposure to experience is
suggested adequately by the formal patterning of the
play. The repetition of situations and the sequence of
incidents in the two halves, the recurrence of similar
snatches of conversation, and the sustained focal passivity
of Bert, all establish this sufficiently, so that the little
verse soliloquy that Miller allows him towards the end[4]
seems not only self-conscious but superfluous, except to
the extent that self-consciousness is in keeping with
Bert's adolescence. The movement, rhythm, and form
of the play have brought out, quietly and without
didacticism, the monotony of the warehouse existence
and the difference between Bert and the rest: it does not
need the elaboration of this coda, which compares badly
with Gus's less pretentious roll-call of the automobiles
of past years that immediately precedes it. The play does
not call for this heightening of language as *The Crucible*
did; though its mood is lyrical, its language need not
be—indeed, ought not to be, because the realistic is as
important an element in it as the lyrical. Both the unity
of mood that it sustains and the passivity of its central
figure dictate its shape: it is a natural one-act play.

A View from the Bridge also began as a one-act drama,
Miller's original explanation being:

I have made the assumption that the audience is like
me and would like to see, for once, a fine, high, always
visible arc of forces moving in full view to a single
explosion.[5]

The expansion of it into a two-act play was carried out
for its London production, and Miller has given his
reasons for the change in his Introduction.[6] One change

that he does not mention is the abandoning of the verse form into which much of the play was originally cast. Often this conversation was effected merely by resetting the original as prose without changing it in any other way. (I shall suggest later that there are reasons for this more valid than mere expediency.) Thus Rodolpho's longer speeches at what is now the beginning of Act II were printed as verse (though Catherine answered in prose) but were verbally identical with the *Collected Plays* text.[7] Elsewhere the changes that were made were greater. The pattern of Alfieri's opening speech was entirely different. After the prose description of his practice (from "My wife has warned me . . ." to "the petty troubles of the poor—and yet. . . .")[8] he continued:

> When the tide is right,
> And the wind blows the sea air against these houses,
> I sit here in my office,
> Thinking it is all so timeless here.
> I think of Sicily, from where these people came,
> The Roman rocks of Calabria,
> Siracusa on the cliff, where Carthaginian and Greek
> Fought such bloody fights. I think of Hannibal,
> Who slew the fathers of these people; Caesar
> Whipping them on in Latin.
> Which is all, of course, ridiculous.
> Al Capone learned his trade on these pavements. . . .

This is much less personal and more relaxed in its detachment than the prose version, where Alfieri's identification of himself as an Italian immigrant and his vision of "another lawyer, quite differently dressed," hearing the same complaints in ancient Sicily, is better prepared for and more immediate in its impact. The parenthetic allusion to Al Capone as "the greatest Carthaginian of all" really says more than does the versified ancient-history passage just quoted. There is also a repetiveness about the verse, despite its occasional felicity:

And yet, when the tide is right,
And the green smell of the sea
Floats through my window,
I must look up at the circling pigeons of the poor,
And I see falcons there,
The hunting eagles of the olden time,
Fierce above Italian forests. . . .

And as the parties tell me what the trouble is
I see cobwebs tearing, Adriatic ruins rebuilding them-
    selves; Calabria;
The eyes of the plaintiff seem suddenly carved,
His voice booming toward me over many fallen stones.

The inference here is that Miller is evolving a heightened form of language which, in the right context, could be tellingly employed. If he is right in thinking that this is not the occasion for it, there is no reason why such an occasion should not later be found, and meanwhile it has maintained the progressive enrichment and variation of style that is evidenced in all his plays.

Rewriting the play enabled Miller, as he himself says, to express more fully the viewpoints of Beatrice and Catherine, and thus to make Eddie less of a monster, and to move back in the direction of greater realism. It is worth examining one example of how this is achieved. The following passage of the original corresponds to the scene which, in the *Collected Plays*, occupies pp. 384–387:

EDDIE: You do your lessons today, Garbo?
CATHERINE: Yeah; I'm way ahead anyway. I just gotta practice from now on.
BEATRICE: She could take it down almost as fast as you could talk already. She's terrific. Read something to her later, you'll be surprised.
EDDIE: That's the way, Katie. You're gonna be all right, kid, you'll see.

CATHERINE [*proudly*]: I could get a job right now, Eddie. I'm not even afraid.

EDDIE: You got time. Wait'll you're eighteen. We'll look up the ads—find a nice company; or maybe a lawyer's office or somethin' like that.

CATHERINE: Oh boy! I could go to work now, my teacher said.

EDDIE: Be eighteen first. I want you to have a little more head on your shoulders. You're still dizzy yet. [*To Beatrice*] Where's the kids? They still outside?

BEATRICE: I put them with my mother for tonight. They'd never go to sleep otherwise. So what kinda cargo you have today?

In the expanded version Catherine has already been offered a job, and she and Beatrice are breaking the news to Eddie. This heightens the dramatic effectiveness and rightly makes the role of Beatrice much more active. Realism is increased by the impression of the world outside that their discussion produces, and by the sense of a normal domestic relationship which is counterpointed by the mounting tension of the argument. The whole scene becomes more impulsive and emotional, and Eddie's objections, by being made less rational and plausible, become more ambivalently motivated; this is nicely brought out (p. 386) by his sudden change of heart and Catherine's impassioned response. Another small, but appropriate, change, by deleting the reference to the children, makes Eddie and Beatrice childless.

These changes improve the play, and the expansion into two acts does not diminish its "fine, high, always visible arc of forces." Synge might make a one-act tragedy out of *Riders to the Sea*, but the greater complexity of Miller's theme demands a more extended treatment. The theme is an unusual one for Miller, and at first sight its preoccupation with incestuous desires and suspicions of homosexuality might suggest Tennessee Williams. It is

almost as though, stung by such generalisations as
Kenneth Tynan's—

> At a time when Miller's plays were growing colder and
> more intellectualised, Williams' blazed hotter and more
> sensuous[9]

—he had deliberately challenged Williams on his own
ground by writing about the Sicilian immigrants whose
passionate obsessions in *The Rose Tattoo* had prompted
Tynan's remark. This, however, is probably no nearer
the truth than is Henry Popkin's suggestion that it was
written "with the evident intention of replying to Kazan,"
who had recently filmed Budd Schulberg's *On the Waterfront*.[10] The social reference of Miller's play is at once far
greater than Williams would want and far less political
than Schulberg's. The betrayal of which Eddie is guilty
is very different from the betrayal in *Waterfront* of a
reformer by a hoodlum, and although Miller's enquiry
into New York delinquency[11] might make a good play,
this is certainly not it. Popkin is right in saying "The
play's main topic has become Eddie's troubles,"[12] but
wrong in implying a Williams-like introspection and
narcissism here. The choric role of Alfieri may recall Tom
in *The Glass Menagerie*: in the first version he began by
bidding the audience "Good evening. Welcome to the
theater," much as Tom's opening speech insists that this
is a play, not a slice of life. But Alfieri is far more detached
from this story in one sense than Tom is from his, and
this marks the distinction between Williams and Miller.
Alfieri represent both the secular and the moral law, the
social forces that Eddie is to reject. He is the principle of
social order that is always dominant in Miller's drama,
and the added emphasis of his choric role sets "Eddie's
troubles" in a wider context. Another writer might have
used a priest in this capacity, as Schulberg uses Father
Barry to befriend his Irish-immigrant longshoremen, but
Miller's choice of a lawyer is significant. In *All my Sons*

Ann's brother George is a lawyer, and so is Bernard in *Death of a Salesman*. Either could have gone into any other profession as far as the story is concerned, for all that is required of them is that they make good; indeed, it might have been better to have George in some other post, for a lawyer might be expected to handle the Keller situation more professionally and less emotionally than he does. But lawyers they are, as though Miller feels a particular symbolism of rightness in the law; for George, Bernard, and Alfieri, with increasing prominence in each successive play, do stand for order and moral justice in a more than professional sense, and it is, of course, that order and moral justice which is betrayed by the theocracy in *The Crucible*. Yet Alfieri cannot avert the disaster that Eddie is bringing on himself, and he admits it in a phrase more revealing than it sounds:

> But I will never forget how dark the room became when he looked at me; his eyes were like tunnels. I kept wanting to call the police, but nothing had happened. Nothing at all had really happened.[13]

Miller's characters are always beyond the help of the police, because what happens to them is not actionable in any ordinary manner. *Focus* opens with an unknown woman calling "Police!" in the night, while Mr Newman finds excuses for not intervening in what is not his affair. Another nocturnal disturbance from which he thinks to escape by simply phoning the police turns out to be something too trivial to call the police to, but all the more frightening because of that.[14] Chris Keller cannot bring himself to call the police to his father: he announces that he will "take him in," but instead gives his father the opportunity of suicide. The ordinary stable world of crime and punishment is always just around the corner in Miller's plays—within call, yet out of reach. These people are their own executioners in obedience to laws more inexorable than those of criminal justice.

This connects with another key phrase in Miller's work, one that Eddie uses with increasing vehemence in the closing minutes of this play: "I want my name!" When John Proctor recants his confession he does so because he refuses to put his name to it; taxed with the illogicality of his position, he breaks out into an impassioned explanation:

> Because it is my name! Because I cannot have another in my life. . . . How may I live without my name? I have given you my soul; leave me my name![15]

This name for which Proctor dies is his moral integrity, not merely his reputation with others, but reputation is an important aspect of it. Thus Abigail's jealousy of her good name in Salem received further emphasis in the revision of that play by the addition of the lines "My name is good in the village! I will not have it said my name is soiled."[16] In *An Enemy of the People* Miller had made Morten Kiil similarly anxious that his name should be kept clean. Willy Loman distinguished, in one of the memorable phrases of *Death of a Salesman*, between being liked and being well liked, but Willy had the wrong values. Miller's preoccupation with the name as reputation and the name as moral integrity suggests another distinction, this time between being known and being wholly known. The reputation, the name that Willy, Kiil, and Abigail have, has some validity, but will not stand up to the fierce scrutiny that John Proctor's or Eddie Carbone's will. Miller commented, as long ago as 1949:

> For, if it is true to say that in essence the tragic hero is intent upon claiming his whole due as a personality, and if this struggle must be total and without reservation, then it automatically demonstrates the indestructible will of man to achieve his humanity.[17]

This certainly fits Proctor well: his whole due as a

personality requires that he retain control of his own conscience and his own destiny.

Because reviewers missed the significance of this in *The Crucible*, Miller tells us, he determined to make it explicit in the next play: "The engaged narrator, in short, appears."[18] It is only in the later version, however, that Alfieri really makes clear Eddie's "will to achieve his humanity." Originally the play had concluded thus:

> Most of the time now we settle for half,
> And I like it better.
> And yet, when the tide is right
> And the green smell of the sea
> Floats in through my window,
> The waves of this bay
> Are the waves against Siracusa,
> And I see a face that suddenly seems carved;
> The eyes look like tunnels
> Leading back toward some ancestral beach
> Where all of us once lived.
> And I wonder at those times
> How much of all of us
> Really lives there yet,
> And when we will truly have moved on,
> On and away from that dark place,
> That world that has fallen to stones?
> This is the end of the story. Good night.

It is not surprising that one critic should have written:

> The play is almost glaringly primitivist, and in feeling, operatic: the right analogy seems not with the Greeks but with Merimée, the Merimée not only of *Carmen* but of *Mateo Falcone*.[19]

The primitive element of the vendetta has already been adequately established by the fight, and Eddie's death constitutes a sufficient criticism of it without this added emphasis. What the re-written curtain speech does is to set the story, not in historical, but in moral perspective, and to lift it above the vendetta story by its insistence on Eddie's moral intransigence:

> Most of the time now we settle for half and I like it better. But the truth is holy, and even as I know how wrong he was, and his death useless, I tremble, for I confess that something perversely pure calls to me from his memory—not purely good, but himself purely, for he allowed himself to be wholly known and for that I think I will love him more than all my sensible clients. And yet, it is better to settle for half, it must be! And so I mourn him—I admit it—with a certain ... alarm.[20]

This is emotive writing which will not be to everyone's taste, but by introducing the important phrases "himself purely, for he allowed himself to be wholly known," this version prevents our seeing Eddie as the animal— which is what Marco has just called him. Alfieri is essential to this play, not because of the obtuseness of the audience (as Miller seems to suggest), but because of the enormity of Eddie's offence against our normal social values. Except to the extent that Alfieri's "certain alarm" with which he mourns Eddie recalls his earlier instinct to call the police, Miller's judgment of Eddie invites us temporarily to suspend our normal values. We see

> that however one might dislike this man, who does all sorts of frightful things, he possesses or exemplifies the wondrous and humane fact that he too can be driven to what in the last analysis is a sacrifice of himself for his conception, however misguided, of right, dignity, and justice.[21]

This is the logical extreme of the position Miller has adopted throughout his work: an almost Transcendentalist insistence on the individual's duty to his own conscience is widened by the non-Transcendentalist recognition that his conscience may mislead him. *A View from the Bridge* is tragic because of Eddie's integrity, sustained to his own destruction against the counsels of his friends and the code of his society. *Death of a Salesman* is not tragic because Willy Loman has no such conception of integrity. He wants to be well-liked, and ignores the moral inconsistencies into which that desire betrays him. Eddie really is "intent upon claiming his whole due as a personality"; he wants his respect (a key word on the lips of several characters here) and sacrifices everything to that. This is a further reason why I am uneasy over Miller's attribution of pure evil to the judges in *The Crucible*: if moral intransigence in Eddie, though misguided, can invite our alarmed admiration, why not their single-minded, if equally misguided, conception of duty? Even if, as educated and religious men, they may be expected to know better than an ignorant longshoreman, their conduct is not necessarily a conscious choice of recognised evil. Character in Miller's plays rests rather on the view of life formulated in these lines of Meredith:

> The wrong is mixed. In tragic life, God wot,
> No villain need be! Passions spin the plot:
> We are betrayed by what is false within.[22]

Miller's grasp of the concept of evil may lead him one day to a play in which that evil is embodied in one man or one group of men fully conscious of their role, but none of his plays so far fits this category.

This play is "a view from the bridge" not only because its setting is Brooklyn, but more importantly because it tries to show all sides of the situation from the detached eminence of the external observer. Alfieri is essential to the play because he is the bridge from which it is seen. (Budd Schulberg's title equally designates the more engaged angle from which he studies life "on the waterfront.") I have already commented on Miller's fondness for imagery of vision and perspective from *Focus* right

H

through his work. The two New York plays that formed this double bill are similarly connected. The transition from the first to the last Monday is effected by Bert and Kenneth with youthful optimism removing the grime of years from the warehouse windows because "it'll be nice to watch the seasons pass."[23] The passing of the seasons, however, brings a change in the ownership of the premises opposite, and when a brothel is established there Kenneth's vestigial decency is stung into protesting to his manager: "I mean to say, it's a terrible disorganizing sight staring a man in the face eight hours a day, sir." The reply has the merit of logic: "Shouldn't have washed the windows, I guess,"[24] but is used ironically by Miller. The moral he really points has been criticised as over-obvious, but it is none the less relevant to a good deal of American drama. If you want to look at views from bridges, to explode the normal façade of a house to see what goes on inside, you must be prepared to accept what you see and to assess it for what it is, not for what you would like it to be. Cleaning windows to watch the seasons may bring a brothel into view as well, but there is no reason to concentrate on either to the exclusion of the other. *A View from the Bridge* may bring unexpectedly into focus the tragic integrity of Eddie Carbone, but it does not minimise the enormity or the ugliness of his betrayal of his family. To express the dualism of this view, Miller's dialogue, blending Eddie's Brooklyn vernacular with the more imaginative speech of Rodolpho and Alfieri, is better than the original poetic idiom would have been, because of its greater realism. The dramatic climaxes of this play, more than of any of his others, do not rely on words, but are passions visualised in action. The intensity of action is often deliberately contrasted with the casualness of the dialogue, as in the sparring scene and the chair-lifting. No words could approach the effect in the theatre of the kiss which Eddie gives Rodolpho and which signals so startlingly his contempt for him. It is a breaking-out, a point of no return, comparable in its theatrical power to Serafina's shattering, in *The Rose Tattoo*, of the urn containing her husband's ashes, or, in a different key, to the window-cleaning in *A Memory of two Mondays*. As with all Miller's plays, there is an effect of great power, of immediacy, and above all of a deeply-felt human concern. The skill of construction is once again allied to a dexterous manipulation of the dramatic lens so as to bring into focus two views of the same sequence of events, and the disciplined handling of elemental passions suggests new potentialities in Miller.

REFERENCES

1. *C.P.*, p. 48.
2. *C.P.*, p. 49. (This is the source also of his next-quoted comments on this play.)
3. *C.P.*, p. 370.
4. *C.P.*, pp. 370–1.
5. Quoted by John Chapman (no source given) in *Theatre '56*, New York 1956, p. 319.
6. *C.P.*, pp. 50–2.
7. This applies to all Rodolpho's speeches from the one beginning "Catherine, if I ever brought you home" (*C.P.*, p. 419) to "Why are you so afraid of him?" (*C.P.*, p. 420). For the text of the first version of this play I have had to depend on the abridgments published in *The Best Plays of 1955–56* and in *Theatre '56* (see n. 5 above).
8. *C.P.*, p. 379.
9. *Encounter*, May 1954, p. 18.
10. *Sewanee*, Winter 1960, p. 39.
11. See p. 10 above.
12. *Sewanee*, Winter 1960, p. 60.
13. *C.P.*, p. 423.
14. *F.*, p. 132.
15. *C.P.*, p. 328.
16. *C.P.*, p. 232.
17. Quoted as from *New York Times* in *Best Plays of 1948–49*, p. 53.
18. *C.P.*, p. 47.
19. Louis Kronenberger, *Best Plays of 1955–56*, p. 13.
20. *C.P.*, p. 439.
21. *C.P.*, p. 51.
22. *Modern Love*, Sonnet No. 43.
23. *C.P.*, p. 357.
24. *C.P.*, p. 369.

CHAPTER VII

THE DRAMA, THE FAMILY AND SOCIETY

One of Miller's avowed reasons for re-writing *A View from the Bridge* was the realisation that its first version "was expressing a very personal preoccupation" and that it embodied a distant analogy to his own psychological life.[1] One possible interpretation of it may at least have the merit of unifying the impressions of his work as a whole that this book has put forward.

To the 1957 edition of this play Miller prefixed a seventeen-page essay "On Social Plays," in which he advances the belief that Greek classical drama succeeded because

> The Greek citizen of that time thought of himself as belonging not to a "nation" or a "state" but to a *polis*. The polis [*sic*] were small units, apparently deriving from an earlier tribal organization, whose members probably knew one another personally because they were relatively few in number and occupied a small territory. . . . The preoccupation of the Greek drama with ultimate law, with the Grand Design, so to speak, was therefore an expression of a basic assumption of the people, who could not yet conceive, luckily, that any man could long prosper unless his polis prospered.[2]

I have already pointed to a preoccupation with ultimate law in *A View from the Bridge*, and the vendetta element there may not unreasonably be described as "deriving from an earlier tribal organization." It has become a critical commonplace that *A View from the Bridge* is an attempt at Greek tragedy, though I do not think that

Miller has given this any support more direct than the publishing of this essay—which contains no specific reference to the play—in the same volume. Eddie, I suggest, belongs to a *polis*, in that the Italian immigrant longshoremen constitute a small unit whose members know one another personally because they are few in number and occupy a small territory, as well as having the memory of something approximating to a tribal organisation in the background. The loyalty to Marco and Rodolpho as "submarines" (unauthorised immigrants) is more than a loyalty to his wife's relations: it is an ethnic loyalty to a self-contained group with common antecedents. This is built up by the introduction of the anecdote of Vinny Bolzano, who betrayed a "submarine" uncle, and of the episode of the two immigrant relatives of Lipari, who have no direct role in the play, as well as by the almost ritualistic attitude of "a certain formal stiffness" that Marco tries to preserve towards Eddie.[3] Thus Eddie's betrayal of the "submarines" is a threat to "the right way to live *together*," which is what Miller regards as the great feature of the *polis*,[4] and in cutting himself off from his *polis* he destroys himself.

To see one sense in which this may constitute a "distant analogy" to Miller's own life we need to consider an earlier short story which had also been concerned with an American-Italian theme. With the exception of "It takes a Thief," a minor semi-humorous story about the dilemma of a car-dealer who is robbed of a vast sum of cash acquired in transactions about which he prefers the police not to know, "Monte Saint Angelo"[5] is the only piece of Miller's creative work that has not already been mentioned. It was published in 1951, and is the story of a young American, Vincent Appello, on holiday in Italy with his friend Bernstein, in quest of relatives and graves of the Appello family. The two friends (like other pairs in Miller's plays) "liked each other not for reasons so much as for possibilities; it was as though they both had

sensed they were opposites." Bernstein is unenthusiastic
about the whole enterprise, bewildered by Appello's
evident satisfaction at a meeting with an aunt who is
unable to understand the situation at all, and impatient
of his friend's unsuccessful search for family tombs. The
more Appello feels himself at home, the more deracinated
Bernstein becomes. Then when they are lunching in a
restaurant, he is attracted to its sole occupant, a man of
peasant stock, who reproaches them for ordering meat on
a Friday. When the stranger is about to leave, he unties
his bundle in order to put in the new loaf he has just
bought:

> Bernstein took a breath. There was something a little
> triumphant, a new air of confidence and superiority
> in his face and voice, as though now for the first time
> it was he who had the private secret and was at home.
> "He's Jewish, Vinny," he said.
>   Vinny turned to look at the man. "Why?"
>   "The way he works that bundle. It's exactly the way
> my father used to tie a bundle. And my grandfather.
> The whole history is packing bundles and getting away.
> Nobody else can be as tender and delicate with bundles.
> That's a Jewish man tying a bundle."

Questioned, the man denies being a Jew and is not even
clear what Jews are ("Are they Catholics? The He-
brews?") Nevertheless he is determined to reach home
with his new bread before sundown, though for no other
conscious reason than that it was his father's custom.
Returning, at Bernstein's suggestion, to the church, the
two friends succeed in finding the Appello tombs and
Bernstein shares Vinny's elation, commenting "I feel
like . . . at home in this place."

> There was an irony in it he could not name. And yet
> pride was running through him like a narrow and
> cool trickle of water. Of what he should be proud he

had no idea; perhaps it was only that under the glacial crush of history a Jew had survived, had been shorn of his consciousness, but still held on to that final impudence of a Saturday Sabbath and a fresh bread.

Delicately and simply told, this story goes to the heart of Miller's work in at least three ways: its sense of wonder, its sense of home, and its sense of the fundamental solidarity of human ties.

It is the third of these that I see as linking it with *A View from the Bridge*. As Bernstein the Jew, observing his Italian-immigrant-friend's sense of *polis*, comes to realise that he, too, has a *polis* even more enduring, if more subtle, so, I suggest, Miller's concern with Eddie accentuates his own sense of conflicting loyalties and at the same time resolves it. I see no evidence for so literal an interpretation of the play as to infer that Miller feels he has betrayed his Jewish heritage. Nostalgia for the *polis* is anachronistic: the goal of the "submarine" is affiliation, through American citizenship, with a larger, more viable community. The essay "On Social Plays" censures the contemporary dramatic obsession with frustration:

The world, I think, is moving toward a unity, a unity won not alone by the necessities of the physical developments themselves, but by the painful and confused re-assertion of man's inherited will to survive.[6]

Such a faith in survival is a direct product of Miller's Jewish heritage ("The whole history is packing bundles and getting away"), strengthened by his observation of the lengths of heroic sacrifice to which men will go if their integrity is absolute.

This also throws light on Miller's preoccupation with "The Family in Modern Drama." That essay was being written at the time when he was re-working *A View from the Bridge*, and latent in that essay is a concept of the family as a *polis*. Miller has never been interested in family plays merely as a means of delineating the affectional ties that link us to our relatives:

> Sentimentalism is perfectly all right, but it is nowhere near a great challenge, and to pursue it . . . is not going to bring us closer to the fated mission of the drama.[7]

This mission of the drama is "to bring us closer to ourselves if only it can grow and change with the changing world." The question that it asks is:

> How may man make for himself a home in that vastness of strangers and how may he transform that vastness into a home?

Or, to use the terms he employs in "On Social Plays," how can man develop for himself a transitional *polis* that may bridge the gap between the private home of the family and the public home of that new unity towards which he believes the world to be moving? For Miller, as for Eliot, although in a different way, "Home is where one starts from." It is not the responsibility of the dramatist to draw up blueprints for a new society, but to give the news of the present: it is the drama's "capacity to open up the present" that Miller stresses in this essay, and if this constitutes an implicit criticism of *A Memory of two Mondays*, it explains his concerns in *A View from the Bridge*. At the time when he was re-writing that play he enunciated this belief:

> It is true to say, I think, that the language of the family is the language of the private life—prose. The language of society, the language of the public life, is verse.[8]

If the textual changes were intended to make the play more domestic, the re-writing of many original verse passages *verbatim* as prose implies a deliberate desire in

this instance to blur the distinction between the private
and the public, and to suggest the shading of one into
the other that this whole view of life postulates.

Miller's family drama has, from *All my Sons* onward,
always tried to make this sort of connexion. It is not that
he uses the family as a microcosm, but rather that, in
"laying siege to the fortress of unrelatedness,"[9] he always
sees the family as related to the larger group, the society,
in inescapable and life-giving ways. In an age when
platitudes about the American woman proliferate, when
generalisations about America as a matriarchal society
have become so prevalent that "Mom-ism" is now a
common usage, it is interesting to see how Miller has
always disdained this crude stereotype. The explanation
of this is not primarily ethnic, nor primarily psychological: Daniel Schneider regards *Death of a Salesman* as
having, for "its basic and hidden motivation",

> the guilt of a younger brother for his hatred of his older
> brother, for Willy Loman is also a younger brother. . . .
> This is the dream of a younger, unpreferred son. No
> other analysis, it seems to me, can account for the
> increasing frequency of the vision of Ben, Willy's older
> and envied brother. In a sense, every first son "strikes
> it rich" in a younger son's eyes.[10]

This is just not true of Hap Loman, or of Chris Keller
(whom Schneider does not mention in this connexion),
both of whom are very much aware of the advantages
they have over their elder brothers, much as they admire
them. Nor is Willy's dream of Ben to be explained quite
so simply: it is in the father-role that we are concerned
with Willy, not as a brother, and Kenneth Tynan's
reminder that Miller is himself a younger brother is not
the whole answer either.[11] Neither the mother nor any
other individual member of the family is given any
artificial eminence by Miller, because he sees the family
as a group. The sons' disillusion in the father in the three

earlier plays brings disaster because of the excessive veneration they have given him (Willy Loman, says Schneider, "is not in the eyes of his sons just a man, but a god in decay"), and because of the circumstances in which that disillusion comes about.

The impulse of the family is towards disintegration, and the play that concentrates on that is likely to be, if not tragic, at least sad. Thus Eugene O'Neill's *Long Day's Journey into Night*, by concentrating on the friction within a family circle of mother, father, and two sons, as in Miller's plays, produces a totally different effect. As in the Loman household, resentment, jealousy, and transferred guilt play havoc with normal relationships, and yet in a curious way there is a stronger solidarity among the four haunted Tyrones. This passage will illustrate my meaning: the father is in the garden talking to a neighbour when the servant is sent to call him to his meal; his elder son comments:

JAMIE: Interrupting the famous Beautiful Voice! She should have more respect.

MARY: It's you who should have more respect! Stop sneering at your father! I won't have it! You ought to be proud you're his son! He may have his faults. Who hasn't? But he's worked hard all his life. He made his way up from ignorance and poverty to the top of his profession! Everyone else admires him and you should be the last one to sneer—you who, thanks to him, have never had to work hard in your life! Remember your father is getting old, Jamie. You really ought to show more consideration.[12]

This is strikingly close to Linda's reproach to her sons, and if it gains by asking for consideration rather than "attention," that is in keeping with the spirit of the play. The claustrophobia that I spoke of in *Death of a Salesman* is something that oppresses Willy but which the other characters do not succumb to in the same way or to the same extent. In the O'Neill play it overwhelms them all equally and the outside world has far less meaning for any of them than it has for the Lomans. The dialogue between Mary and her sons continues thus, after she tells Jamie he ought to show more consideration:

JAMIE: *I* ought to?

EDMUND: Oh, dry up, Jamie. And for Pete's sake, Mama, why jump on Jamie all of sudden?

MARY: Because he's always sneering at someone else, always looking for the worst weakness in everyone. But I suppose life has made him like that, and he can't help it. None of us can help the things life has done to us.

The complexity of this exchange, which comes out vividly on the stage, lies in the readiness of each to spring to the defence of, and find excuses for, a member of the family whom they were themselves attacking a moment earlier and will again attack when the others are not doing so. The centripetal force that holds this family together and gives the play its dramatic impetus is suggested by the euphemism they all use to describe one another's weakness: Jamie in his drunkenness or Mary in her drug-taking is said to have "gone far away from us." The note of separation this introduces is an important one in the melody of the play as a whole. There is a dominant tenderness here, for what might otherwise become an intolerably prolonged family altercation is constantly broken by the fumbled apology, the immediate regret for hasty words, the desire to soften the blow even while the blow is being delivered.

In a Miller family the force is not centripetal but centrifugal. This results in a dissolution that is no less painful than the Tyrones' cohesion, but ultimately more regenerative for the individual. Mary's lament for "the things life has done to us" contrasts sharply with a *motif* recurrent in Miller's plays that is expressed in its clearest form in this speech from *The Man who had all the Luck*: Hester is fighting against David's determinist superstition:

> Stand here, Davey! Don't go out. You are the lightning, you are the banging hail! Do you see it, do you understand what happened? You are the god now; there was nothing in the sky that gave you things, nothing that could take them away! It was always you, Davey.

This is far more than a crude assertion of American individualism. The individual who can survive the inevitable disintegration of the family and who can find for himself another role in the larger social group can become "at home in the world" in a way that is impossible to the Tyrones whose roles are wholly familial.

This view of the family has a bearing on another criticism of Miller that is voiced from time to time. Henry Popkin epitomises it: "On the whole, Miller's implicit indictment of sex as a wicked influence is remarkably consistent and emphatic."[13] This is misleading in some respects, for it does not apply at all to *The Man who had all the Luck* nor to *All my Sons*: it would be distorting the theme of that play to attribute the catastrophe to Chris's love for Ann simply because her return occasions the dénouement. "Please don't kill Anything" and the expanded version of *The Misfits* both appeared after Mr Popkin's article, but the influence of the girl in both (especially in the second) is anything but wicked. What is criticised in Miller's plays is sex in its anti-family and anti-social manifestations. Willy's sordid liaison with the woman in Boston, Hap's seduction of the executives' fiancées, John Proctor's adultery with Abigail, Eddie Carbone's incestuous promptings towards Catherine— all these are destructive manifestations of sex as an undisciplined passion menacing alike the integrity of the man and the solidarity of the family. Against these must be set, in the same plays, not only the love of Catherine and Rodolpho, but also the confidence in marriage as a satisfactory partnership when both partners are prepared to make it so. This social concern may inhibit a more ecstatically romantic attitude to love, but sex is never so consistently and emphatically wicked an influence in Miller's plays as it is in *A Streetcar named Desire*, *Summer and Smoke*, or Tennessee Williams's plays in general. It is never the consuming fire that it is in Williams's work, but neither is it the same totally corrupting influence. Willy's extra-marital adventures do not liberate him, but they do not corrupt him either; and if Biff is destroyed in the process, it is by the discovery of his father's imperfection, not directly by sex. The implicit condemnation of the Boston stocking-party is as a betrayal of Linda and Biff, not of Willy.

Miller's most mature and complex treatment of sex to date is in the expanded version of *The Misfits*. His presentation of Roslyn as a woman in love is done with feeling, but with an interesting economy and indirectness of method. Miller is characteristically less concerned with a study of feminine psychology than with mirroring, in her effect upon the three men, the impact that love has on her. It is ultimately a regenerative passion, but only when she has conquered fear and fought Gay into an acceptance of her values and her belief in life. She is important in another respect, too, for her spontaneity, her vitality, and her sense of wonder are qualities that Miller has always valued but seldom dramatised so effectively. Her antecedents are to be found, not in any of his woman-characters, but in his description of Thomas Stockmann in *An Enemy of the People*:

He might be called the eternal amateur—a lover of things, of people, of sheer living, a man for whom the days are too short, and the future fabulous with discoverable joys. And for all this most people will not like

him—he will not compromise for less than God's own
share of the world while they have settled for less than
Man's.[14]

If the same description might, in some respects, be applied
to Miller himself, it would be necessary to complete it by
referring to other elements in *The Misfits* as well. *Esquire*
captioned it, on its first appearance, "The Last Frontier
of the Quixotic Cowboy"; and a prominent note in the
expanded version also is this sense of the disappearance
of the American Dream. The cowboys of this story, while
responding to the wild beauty of the mountain scenery,
constantly contrast with it a memory of the days when
the frontier was wilder still and when the mustang herds
were larger. Striking a balance between the falsely-tough
and the facilely-sentimental, Miller tempers their nos-
talgic wonder with a real feeling of loss which is partly
due to the passage of time, partly to the inadequacy
of man to his opportunities, partly to the inability of
deracinated man to make a home for himself in the world.
    And yet, coexistent with this, the wonder in Miller
still survives. People who know only *Death of a Salesman*
would be baffled by the suggestion that a sense of wonder
is the strongest impulse behind his work, but the suggestion can be supported by far more evidence than merely
the frequency with which he applies the word to his own
aims.[15] The wonder at the possibilities of life that gives
vividness to "Monte Saint Angelo" and to "A Boy Grew
in Brooklyn" is paralleled in a delightful essay on "The
American Theatre."[16] This is really a projection of
Miller's enthusiasm for his vocation and an attempt to
communicate the excitement and the glamour of the
theatre which always transcends and justifies the strains
and disappointments that he also evokes. But wonder is a
better stimulus for the creative writer than for the critic,
and Miller's criticism, though it is always interesting, is
uneven. The introduction to the *Collected Plays* is the

product of a fascination with process; it is the story of
how the plays came to be written, and all the time Miller
seems surprised that it was really he who wrote them.
His discussion of other people's plays forms a smaller
part of his critical work, and his remarks on, for example,
The Cocktail Party and *Cat on a Hot Tin Roof* are generous
and perceptive without offering any major new evaluation.[17] Miller, of course, never claims to be making anything more than subjective observations, and his critical
essays are marked by a modesty that prevents sincerity of
belief from being inflated into *ex cathedra* dogmatism.
Similarly his comments on his own work are often self-
reproachful rather than self-critical. The popular image
of Miller as an intellectual, while it has real basis in fact,
must not lead to the expectation of major contributions
to critical theory, at least in the essays so far published.
Their value (and it is by no means inconsiderable) lies
in the candour of their insight into his own creative process and his own standards.

The sense of wonder in which the plays originate is
illustrated by Miller's method of working as described by
his friend Alan Seager.[18] He begins by filling notebooks
with random jottings (of which Seager produces ex-
amples). They may comprise:

aphorisms, scraps of dialogue invented or recalled,
short or long poems left incomplete, drawings of sets
for as-yet-unconceived plays, personal memoranda in
which he talks to himself or asks himself the meaning
of some dream or childhood incident, spurts of plotting
which may suddenly reveal a whole act, or with luck,
the beginning, middle and end of a play.

Among this detritus of wonder at the inexhaustible
multiplicity of experience occur such pieces of self-
advice as "Beware following the details to the loss of
vision," followed by "Beware following the vision to the
loss of details." Vision in both senses of the word is

central to Miller's creativity: when it has been brought satisfactorily into focus there comes the moment when, in his own words, "thinking is left behind. Everything is in the present tense and a play emerges which has resemblances but little else to the mass of notes left behind."

It is in this way that Miller comes "to make something of existence."[19] The unusual range of the periodicals listed in our bibliography as containing articles on or by him is a measure of the interest his work has aroused in widely different circles. It is a tribute, not so much to his technical accomplishment or to his commitment to any formulated ideology, as to his firm grasp on the things that matter. Never as committed as is sometimes supposed to the processes of politics, Miller has become more and more concerned with the processes of living, at the same time as his command of language and powers of construction have been developing. He has recently said:

> I am not calling for more ideology. . . . I am simply asking for a theatre in which an adult who wants to live can find plays that will heighten his awareness of what living in our time involves. I am tired of a theatre of sensation, that's all. I am tired of seeing man as merely a bundle of nerves. That way lies pathology, and we have pretty well arrived.[20]

The only conclusion to which an interim progress report of this nature can fairly come is one of confidence in Miller's proven ability to develop still further the range and depth of his wonder at the complexity and potentiality of human nature and human existence. At the heart of all his work is a salutary restlessness of spirit and a zest for experience. These have been and can be again harnessed for a dramatic power far greater than the indignation of protest to which critics have so often tried to reduce his plays.

REFERENCES

1. *C.P.*, p. 50.
2. *V.B.*, pp. 1–2.
3. *C.P.*, pp. 388–9, 429–31, 391.
4. *V.B.*, p. 6.
5. In *Harper's Magazine*, Mar. 1951, pp. 39–47.
6. *V.B.*, p. 16.
7. "F.M.D.," pp. 40–1.
8. "F.M.D.," p. 38.
9. *C.P.*, p. 19.
10. *Theatre Arts*, Oct. 1949, p. 21.
11. *Encounter*, May 1954, p. 14.
12. Eugene O'Neill, *Long Day's Journey into Night*, New Haven 1956, pp. 60–1.
13. *Sewanee Review*, Winter 1960, p. 56.
14. *E.P.*, p. 23.
15. *e.g.*, *C.P.*, p. 15.
16. *Holiday*, Jan. 1955.
17. In, respectively, "F.M.D." and "The Shadows of the Gods."
18. *Lilliput*, January 1960, pp. 30–3.
19. See p. 26 above.
20. "The State of the Theatre," in *Harper's Magazine* 221 (Nov. 1960), p. 66.

NEW YORK PRODUCTIONS OF THE PLAYS

The Man who had all the Luck: 4 performances, Forest Theatre, 23–25 Nov. 1944. Produced by Herbert H. Harris; staged by Joseph Fields; setting by Frederick Fox.

All my Sons: 328 performances, Coronet Theatre, 29 Jan.–8 Nov. 1947. Produced by Harold Clurman, Elia Kazan, and Walter Fried, in association with Herbert H. Harris; staged by Elia Kazan; setting by Mordecai Gorelik. Awarded New York Drama Critics' Prize.

Death of a Salesman: 742 performances, Morosco Theatre, 10 Feb. 1949–18 Nov. 1950. Produced by Kermit Bloomgarden and Walter Fried; staged by Elia Kazan; settings by Jo Mielziner; incidental music by Alex North. Awarded New York Drama Critics' Prize and Pulitzer Prize.

An Enemy of the People (adaptation of Ibsen): 36 performances, Broadhurst Theatre, 28 Dec. 1950–27 Jan. 1951. Produced by Lars Nordenson; staged by Robert Lewis; settings by Aline Bernstein.

The Crucible: 197 performances, Martin Beck Theatre, 22 Jan.–11 Jul. 1953. Produced by Kermit Bloomgarden; staged by Jed Harris; settings by Boris Aronson. Awarded the Antoinette Perry and the Donaldson Prizes.

A Memory of two Mondays and *A View from the Bridge*: 149 performances, Coronet Theatre, 29 Sep. 1955–4 Feb. 1956. Produced by Kermit Bloomgarden and Whitehead Stevens; staged by Martin Ritt; settings by Boris Aronson.

After the Fall: Repertory Theatre of Lincoln Centre, 23 Jan. 1964. Staged by Elia Kazan; setting by Jo Mielziner.

Incident at Vichy: Repertory Theatre of Lincoln Centre, 3 Dec. 1964. Staged by Harold Clurman; setting by Boris Aronson.

BIBLIOGRAPHY

Note

In all cases in which two or more editions of any work are listed, references in the text are to those marked * in this Bibliography. *C.P.* = Miller's *Collected Plays*, New York 1957 and London 1958.

I. ARTHUR MILLER'S PRINCIPAL WORKS

1. Plays

The Man who had all the Luck: in *Cross-section, 1944*, ed. E. Seaver, New York 1944.

All my Sons: New York 1947; Harmondsworth (Penguin) 1961. Also in * *C.P.*

Death of a Salesman: New York (Viking) 1949; London (Cresset) 1949; with expanded initial description and stage directions, New York (Bantam) 1951; New York (Viking Compass) 1958; Harmondsworth (Penguin) 1961. Also in *Four Modern Plays*, New York (Rinehart) 1957; and in * *C.P.*

An Enemy of the People (adaptation of Ibsen's play): * New York (Viking) 1951. Also in *Four Plays of Our Time*, ed. H. Voaden, London 1960.

The Crucible: New York (Viking) 1953). Also * (with an additional scene, subsequently omitted) in *Theatre Arts*, Oct. 1953; and * (with revised text), in *C.P.*

A View from the Bridge, and *A Memory of two Mondays*: New York (Viking) 1955. *A View from the Bridge* (revised text, with an essay "On Social Plays," but without *A Memory of two Mondays*)*: London (Cresset) 1957; (with *All my Sons*) Harmondsworth (Penguin) 1961. Both plays (*View* and *Memory*) also in * *C.P.*

Collected Plays (with introduction): * New York (Viking) 1957; with identical pagination, * London (Cresset) 1958.

2. Prose Fiction

Situation Normal: New York (Reynal) 1944.

Focus: New York (Reynal) 1945; New York (Forum) 1947; London (Gollancz) 1949; London (Ace) 1958, repr. * 1960.

"It takes a Thief," in *Collier's*, New York, 8 Feb. 1947, pp. 23, 75–6.

"Monte Saint Angelo," in *Harper's Magazine*, New York, Mar. 1951, pp. 39–47.

"The Misfits," in *Esquire*, New York, Oct. 1957, pp. 158–66.

"Please don't kill Anything," in *The Noble Savage*, New York (Meridian), No. 1 (1960), pp. 126–31.

The Misfits (comprising film-script in novel form, with original short story of same title listed above): New York (Dell) 1961; (without original short story) Harmondsworth (Penguin) 1961.

3. Miscellaneous Essays, etc.

"A Modest Proposal for the Pacification of Public Temper," in *The Nation*, CLXXIX (3 Jul. 1954), pp. 5–8.

"The American Theatre," in *Holiday*, XVII (Jan. 1955); repr. in *The Passionate Playgoer*, ed. George Oppenheimer, New York 1958.

"A Boy grew in Brooklyn," in *Holiday*, XVII (Mar. 1955).

"The Family in Modern Drama," in *Atlantic*, CXCVII (Apr. 1956), pp. 35–41.

"*Death of a Salesman*: A Symposium," in *The Tulane Drama Review*, New Orleans, II (May 1958), pp. 63–9.

"The Shadows of the Gods: A Critical View of the American Theater," in *Harper's Magazine*, CCXVII (Aug. 1958), pp. 35–43.

"The State of the Theatre: A Conversation with Arthur Miller," reported by Henry Brandon, in *Harper's Magazine*, CCXXI (Nov. 1960), pp. 63–9; repr. in H. Brandon, *As we are*, New York 1961.

II. OTHERS

1. General

DOWNER, ALAN S.: *Fifty Years of American Drama 1900–1950*, Chicago 1951.

GASSNER, JOHN: *The Theatre in Our Times*, New York 1954.

KRUTCH, JOSEPH WOOD: *American Drama Since 1918*. First pub. 1939; * revised and enlarged edn., London 1957.

2. Essays

HUNT, ALBERT: "Realism and Intelligence: Some Notes on Arthur Miller," in *Encore*, London, VII (May–Jun. 1960), pp. 12 ff.

POPKIN, HENRY: "Arthur Miller: The Strange Encounter," in *The Sewanee Review*, LXVIII (Winter 1960), pp. 34 ff.

SEAGER, ALAN: "The Creative Agony of Arthur Miller," in *Lilliput*, XLVI (Jan. 1960).

TYNAN, KENNETH: "American Blues: The Plays of Arthur Miller and Tennessee Williams," in *Encounter*, II (May 1954), pp. 13 ff.

WILLIAMS, RAYMOND: "The Realism of Arthur Miller," in *Critical Quarterly*, I (Summer 1959), pp. 140 ff.

Note

Additions to this bibliography will be found in the Preface to this volume.